Urban Sprawl, Global Warming,
and the Empire of Capital

MONTGOMERY COLLEGE
ROCKVILLE CAMPUS LIBRARY
ROCKVILLE, MARYLAND

# Urban Sprawl, Global Warming, and the Empire of Capital

George A. Gonzalez

PRESS

982039

DEC 2 2 2009

Published by
State University of New York Press, Albany

© 2009 State University of New York

All rights reserved

Printed in the United States of America

No part of this book may be used or reproduced in any manner whatsoever
without written permission. No part of this book may be stored in a retrieval system
or transmitted in any form or by any means including electronic, electrostatic,
magnetic tape, mechanical, photocopying, recording, or otherwise
without the prior permission in writing of the publisher.

For information, contact State University of New York Press, Albany, NY
www.sunypress.edu


Production by Kelli W. LeRoux
Marketing by Anne M. Valentine


Library of Congress Cataloging-in-Publication Data

Gonzalez, George A., 1969–
  Urban sprawl, global warming, and the empire of capital / George A. Gonzalez.
    p. cm.
  Includes bibliographical references and index.
  ISBN 978-0-7914-9389-2 (hardcover : paper)
  1. City planning—United States.   2. Regional planning—United States.   3. Cities
and towns—United States—Growth—Environmental aspects.   4. Geopolitics—
United States.   5. Real estate development—United States.   6. Urban economics—
United States.   I. Title.
  HT384.U5G66 2009
  307.1'2160973—dc22
                                                                                    2009001477

10 9 8 7 6 5 4 3 2 1

# Contents

# Acknowledgments

I am very fortunate to be able to stand on the shoulders of such intellectual giants as G. William Domhoff, Clyde W. Barrow, and John S. Dryzek. I would also like to express my appreciation to my colleagues who took part in the Politics Workshop here at the University of Miami. Chapters of this book were helpfully debated and dissected in this venue. My wife Ileana also deserves my great appreciation. Her love and support energize me and inspire me to struggle for a just and environmentally healthy world. It is to her and our children—my ten-year-old stepson, Roman, and my four-year-old daughter, Alana—that I dedicate this book. It is also dedicated to all the generations that have to pay the costs for the reckless treatment of earth's natural resources and its biosphere. It is my deeply felt hope that this book contributes in some small way to humanity's successful adaptation to the limits of the environment.

Portions of this book appeared earlier in my articles: "An Eco-Marxist Analysis of Oil Depletion via Urban Sprawl," *Environmental Politics* 15, no. 4 (August 2006): 515–31; "Urban Sprawl, Global Warming, and the Limits of Ecological Modernization," *Environmental Politics* 14, no. 3 (June 2005): 344–62. Work from these articles is reprinted with permission of the publisher (Taylor and Francis Ltd, http://www.tandf.co.uk/journals). My article "An Eco-Marxist Analysis of Oil Depletion via Urban Sprawl" was reprinted in the edited volume *Political Theory and Global Climate Change* (Cambridge: MIT Press, 2008) under the title "Urban Sprawl, Climate Change, Oil Depletion, and the Eco-Marxism."

Also, portions of chapter 6 were drawn from "Democratic Ethics and Ecological Modernization: The Formulation of California's Automobile Emission Standards," *Public Integrity* 4, no. 4 (Fall 2001): 325–44. Copyright © 2001 by M. E. Sharpe, Inc. Reprinted with permission. All rights reserved. Not for reproduction.

# Chapter One

# Urban Sprawl and the Empire of Capital

The United States is a global leader in the anthropogenic emission of the key greenhouse gas—carbon dioxide. It is responsible for roughly 25 percent of the globe's anthropogenic emission of this gas.[1] Moreover, the United States is the leading per capita emitter of carbon dioxide.[2] On a per person, or per capita, basis, it emits a great deal more of this gas than European countries, including Russia, and than China, Japan, and South Korea (Revkin 2001; Lanne and Liski 2004; Baumert, Herzog, and Pershing 2005, 20; Kramer 2005; United Nations Framework Convention on Climate Change 2006; Greenwatch 2007; International Energy Agency 2007). The role of the United States as a prime cause of the planet's warming is neither coincidental nor readily remedied. Instead, the U.S. role in the global warming trend is the result of the operation of the global economy, and the special role that the United States plays within it.

More specifically, it is the urban sprawl in the United States that has important implications for both climate change and the world economy. Beginning especially in the post–World War II period, diffuse urban development in the United States became the means to absorb the increasing productive capacities of the world's industrial base. Urban sprawl aids in the consumption of industrial output, because it increases demand for automobiles. Also, because housing developments on the urban periphery tend to produce relatively large single-family homes, such housing generally requires more appliances, furniture, and other consumer goods than smaller abodes (e.g., those within apartment complexes).

While urban sprawl serves as an important spur for the global economy, it is also a key factor behind the massive amounts of carbon dioxide emitted by the U.S. economy. Urban sprawl necessitates the usage of relatively large amounts of energy. This energy is needed for the long

1

commuting distances via automobiles required in the context of diffuse urban development (Banister 2005). Also, the heating and cooling of spacious suburban homes requires substantial amounts of energy, as does the powering of appliances in multiroom single-family homes.[3] The huge energy needs created by urban sprawl in the United States have been mostly met by the burning of fossil fuels. These fuels when burned for energy emit carbon dioxide.[4]

Why have U.S. urban areas become so sprawled, and an important cause of global warming? The answer to this question can be predominately found in the political and economic behavior of economic elites and producer groups. A geopolitical factor facilitating the sprawling of U.S. urban zones has been the United States' historic access to abundant supplies of fossil fuels.

I begin this chapter by outlining two different views on the operation of the global economy. The proponents of the first view outlined, termed by me the globalization thesis, emphasize the market, international political organizations, and multinational corporations in their analysis of the world economy. Conversely, as these factors have gained preeminence globally, the political and economic role of nation-states has been greatly diminished. The second view of the global economy outlined here is labeled by Ellen Meiksins Wood "empire of capital." Unlike the adherents of the globalization thesis, Wood holds that states within the contemporary world economy play a central and vital role. Given the role of the U.S. state in fostering urban sprawl (described below), the pattern of urban development in the U.S. (with its attending economic consequences) lends support to Wood's empire of capital argument. I conclude this chapter by providing an overview of the book.

## THE GLOBALIZATION THESIS

It has recently become vogue for both politicians and academicians to deemphasize the role of the nation-state in the operation of the global economy. Among these thinkers, the world economy is cast as an increasingly stateless system where production and distribution take place with little government involvement. Moreover, it is common for researchers, along with some right-wing populists (e.g., Pat Buchanan), to argue that political power in the global system has shifted from states to transnational political organizations, such as the World Bank, the World Trade Organization, and the International Monetary Fund. Robert Paehlke (2003), for instance, in his analysis of the environmental, economic, and social impacts of the international economy, maintains that the paramount challenge for proponents of democracy is to democratize those global political institutions that oversee and regulate the world's economy.

Other scholars, most prominently William I. Robinson (2004), Leslie Sklair (2001), Kees Van der Pijl (1999), and Susan Strange (1996) contend that political power in the global economy has shifted to groups and individuals that hold key decision-making power within transnational firms. Robinson, for example, identifies what he describes as a transnational capitalist class (TCC) as the new center of power in what can be most accurately termed a global society. For Robinson, the TCC has supplanted the system of political and economic power that characterized international relations beginning with the second industrial revolution until the end of the cold war. During this period, political and economic relations within the capitalist camp were marked by multiple centers of political and economic power rooted in nation-states.

With the advent of the neoliberal political and economic project in the 1980s and 1990s, spearheaded by the United States (Hunt 2007, ch. 8), political and economic relations in the capitalist world began to dramatically change (Duménil and Lévy 2004). Proponents and champions of the neoliberal program argue that the movement of capital, goods, and services should be facilitated throughout the world. Along these lines, neoliberal advocates contend that trade barriers should be lowered/eliminated and countries should move away from dictatorships and toward limited democracies. The advantage of democracies for neoliberal proponents is that democratic governments tend to be more transparent and accessible to global firms than dictatorships. Additionally, those nationalist sentiments that normally inhere within the military of a country tend to be more influential and decisive within a dictatorship. Such sentiments militate against open political and economic regimes. These new democracies, however, are limited insofar as they do not tamper with the economic policies brought about by neoliberalism (Robinson 1996).

It is the economic changes brought about by the neoliberal project that are most closely associated with it, and that are most controversial. It is argued by advocates of neoliberalism that in order to improve the fiscal conditions of governments in developing regions, increase global economic efficiency, expand economic opportunities, and improve economic performance, countries throughout the world should allow for the free movement of capital, goods, and services. Nations are encouraged to reduce tariffs, eliminate subsidies of all types, and generally adopt congenial policies toward international private investors (Gilpin 1987; Stilwell 2002; Bhagwati 2004; Patterson and Afilalo 2008).

In many instances these neoliberal reforms are codified in regional trade agreements (e.g., the North American Free Trade Agreement [NAFTA]), in loan agreements with the World Bank and International Monetary Fund, or historically through the global trade treaty known as the General Agreement on Trade and Tariff (GATT). The primary purpose of the World Trade Organization is to determine if countries' policies are abiding by globally negotiated terms of trade (formerly known as GATT). Organizations such as the World Bank and the International Monetary Fund loan money to countries in order to foster economic activity, and/or to help governments remain solvent.

To run afoul of the World Trade Organization, the International Monetary Fund, and/or the World Bank creates the definite possibility that a country will be economically isolated. It may be denied access to key markets, and the financing needed in the exporting and importing of goods and services. This could be particularly devastating for nations in the developing world, whereby the most important markets for these countries' goods and services are in the developed world and whose productive capacity is vitally dependent on inputs from other countries. The seeming result for a nation that has a falling-out with these global organizations would be economic stagnation, if not depression, and numerous sources of international investment and credit would likely shun it (e.g., Argentina [MacLachlan 2006]). Other results would ostensibly be increasing rates of unemployment and poverty, as well as political instability. Given these possibilities, getting and staying within the good graces of these key international institutions appears to be less an option and more a requisite for most countries of the world.

The result of the political and economic changes brought about by the neoliberal project is to give transnational firms a maximum amount of leverage over the countries of the world. In the contemporary world, capital has a substantial amount of mobility. Given advances in production techniques, means of transportation, and information transmission, firms can shift economic activity all over the world in a very short time frame—sometimes virtually instantaneously. This results in part from the fact that many companies distribute their production infrastructure throughout the globe (Robinson 2004; Friedman 2005). This mobility allows firms to seek out those circumstances that provide for the most favorable environment for profit maximization. As a result, nation-states must strive to provide such an environment if they are going to attract and, just as importantly, maintain the capital investments that foster employment and economic growth in their economy. In this context of maximum capital mobility the effect of neoliberalism is to disempower countries. In other words, neoliberal reforms have resulted in the configuration of governments throughout the world into institutions that can only minimally affect capital flows and investment decisions (Shambaugh 2004).

Significantly, the mobility of capital and the neoliberal reforms enacted throughout the developing world have profoundly affected those nations with developed economies. With neoliberalism creating greater political and economic stability for investors throughout the Third World, such investors can place their money in many regions without concern that governments are going to act against their investments, limit their profit margins, or suddenly increase their operating costs. This, coupled with the fact that labor costs are dramatically lower in many parts of the developing world than in the developed world, has resulted in substantial production infrastructure being retired in the First World and reconstituted in the Third World. Glaringly, a great deal of the U.S. industrial base has been shifted to China, were labor costs are greatly lower than in the United States (Gallagher 2005; Gallagher 2006; Uchitelle 2006; Goodman 2008 August 24). What this demonstrates is that governments in the developed world must strive to create favorable investment climates, much like those in the developing countries. More precisely, developed countries must seek to proximate the cost factors in the developing world, including lower labor and regulatory costs. Hence, capital's newfound mobility and neoliberalism have put the developed world in direct competition with developing nations (Wriston 1992; Castells (1996/1998; Greider 1997; Ohmae 1999; Tonelson 2000; Hardt and Negri 2000; Friedman 2005; Hansen 2006; Prasad 2006). This works to the strategic advantage of transnational firms and, more precisely, their ownership—the TCC.

Robinson, in particular, holds that the owners and managers of transnational firms can be considered as an increasingly coherent class or unit because of the trend toward centralization of ownership over multinational conglomerates, interlocking directorates (whereby firms share the same board of director members), and the coordination of corporate operations through strategic alliances and other forms of cooperation, such as licensing agreements and shared representation within particular countries. The result is that more and more centralized blocs of capital compete between one another over resources and markets. This trend is evident in the oil industry, where over the last few years a series of mergers and acquisitions has significantly narrowed the number of major oil firms (Mouawad 2005). Robinson (2004) explains that the result is a "*transnational* concentration and centralization of capital, that is, the increasing centrality of transnational capital to the world capitalist system." With this increasing concentration of capital, nation-states have less room to maneuver between a lower number of corporate managers and owners who control vast amounts of capital, production expertise, marketing know-how, and distribution networks. Therefore, "Transnational conglomerates now compete against each other . . . and states are indeed overwhelmed by the pressures placed on them by transnational capital" (62).

In the globalizing economy, political power has effectively been transferred away from states and those economic and political interests that surround them, and toward supranational political institutions (i.e., the World Trade Organization, etc.) and increasingly centralized transnational capitalist groupings (i.e., the TCC). This is at least according to those who hold that economic and political power is largely, if not entirely, global in form and operation.

# EMPIRE OF CAPITAL

The most explicit argument against the characterization of the global economic system as operating largely beyond the influences of states is proffered by Ellen Meiksins Wood (1999; 2003). Wood holds that the state, abstractly speaking, plays a much more important role within the context of the global economy than allowed for by advocates and supporters of the globalization thesis. Firstly, the apparent separation of the state from the operation of the economy is an illusion created by the nature of capitalism. Secondly, when consumption, as opposed to production, within the global economy is examined the importance of the state, especially in the developed world, becomes apparent.

## THE STATE AND CAPITALIST PRODUCTION

Capitalism as a system of economic expropriation is different from earlier systems of expropriation insofar as it does not rely directly on extra-economic force to extract surplus value. In economic systems characterized by feudalism or slavery, political/military force is exercised to directly obtain from feudal peasants and slaves the products of their work. In this way extra-economic power is used by political/economic elites to appropriate surplus value from subjugated feudal peasants/slaves, who otherwise directly possess the factors of production (e.g., land). Surplus value represents the amount of economic value beyond what is deemed necessary to reproduce a worker, both in terms of a current worker and future workers (i.e., the offspring of workers). Reflective of the political economy analysis of Karl Marx, Wood explains that within capitalism the object of control is not the product of a worker, but the labor of the worker itself. As a result, the goal of elites (or in this case capitalists) within capitalism is not to directly control the peasants or slaves and force them to turn over the product of their labor for less than its value, but to get workers to sell their labor below its economic worth. For this, capitalists can rely on the market.

A labor market can be managed to ensure that the supply of workers exceeds demand and thus labor costs are pushed down to the point where the amount of economic value created by a worker exceeds the remuneration (i.e., wages) paid that same worker (Hernandez 2002; Light 2006). Therefore, the recently accelerated move toward shifting production toward places like China does not represent a new phase of capitalist development, but is part of a continuing effort on the part of capitalist firms to expand the labor pool, in this case by tapping new labor pools made accessible by technological advances and political changes throughout the developing world (Glyn 2006).

In comparing the mode of capitalist production to earlier modes of production it becomes apparent that within feudalism and slavery the goal for elites was to alienate laborers from the product of their labor, and within capitalism the goal is to alienate workers from the means of production (i.e., factories, farms, as well as distribution and information networks). By legally (and coercively [Sexton 1991; Acher 2001, 2008]) separating workers from the means of production, workers must sell their labor in order to survive. Just as importantly, the labor market has historically operated in such a way that the price of labor has largely been advantageous for capitalists. What is significant for this discussion is to note the centrality of extra-economic force for all three economic systems. The only real difference is that extra-economic force plays a more obvious and direct role in the feudal and slavery systems, because expropriation is carried out through its direct application. In the case of capitalism extra-economic power is employed to ensure that workers remain alienated from the means of production. Put another way, extra-economic force is deployed to establish and maintain the capitalist's control of the means of production.[5]

## CONSUMPTION WITHIN THE GLOBAL ECONOMY

Some within the globalization camp would largely agree with Wood on the role of states in maintaining the socioeconomic structure within the global economy. William Avilés (2006), for instance, relies heavily on Robinson's theory of global politics to analyze the ongoing Colombian civil war, and the political and economic changes made within the context of this conflict. The Colombian civil war pits Marxist/Maoist-inspired rebels against the government. Where there appears to be a clearer break between Wood's thesis of capitalist empire and the globalization perspective is when the consumption side of the global economy is considered. Wood holds that in the final analysis the uneven distribution of wealth and income in the world decisively upends any contention that the world economy operates as a fully integrated economic unit, as inherent in the globalization position (also see Kütting 2004). She (2003) expresses this position in the following:

> Let us accept that the speed and extent of capital movements, especially those that depend on the new information and communication technologies, have created something new. Let us even accept that the world is more "interdependent," at least in the

sense that the effects of economic movement in the heartlands of capital are felt throughout the globe. There remains one overriding indication that the global market is still far from integrated: the fact that wages, prices and conditions of labor are still so widely diverse throughout the world. In a truly integrated market, market imperatives would impose themselves universally, to compel all competitors to approximate some common social average of labor productivity and costs, in order to survive in conditions of price competition. (135–36)

When one considers the deep (and persistent) disparities in wealth and income between the developed and developing worlds ("The Chips are Down" 2002; Firebaugh and Goesling 2004; Bardhan, Bowles, and Wallerstein 2006; Kong 2006), the contemporary global economic system looks less like the result of the free play of markets, and more like the result of an imperial project. It is a system complete with a center, semi-periphery, and periphery, which characterizes all imperial formations. In all of these formations, the center extracts wealth and income from the semi-periphery and periphery, thereby enriching the center—especially the upper socioeconomic strata of the center (Wallerstein 1974/1980; Braudel 1982/1984; Moore 2003; Nexon and Wright 2007). In this context, the U.S. military, with its ability to project overwhelming force throughout the world, takes on the characteristics of the preeminent military power enforcing and maintaining a global economic system that has been historically advantageous to the developed countries (Todd 2003; Agnew 2005; Barrow 2005; D. Harvey 2005; Barkawi 2006). Current U.S. spending on its military roughly equals the current military spending of all the countries of the world combined (Moore 2004; Bacevich 2005; Greenberg and Page 2005, 545; Karen 2005; *SIPRI Yearbook* 2007; Shanker 2008 Feb. 4).

## URBAN SPRAWL IN THE GLOBAL ECONOMY

The importance of urban sprawl becomes clear when we consider consumption within the global economy. Urban sprawl is central to sustaining the empire of capital, and to understanding its modern operation. Importantly, urban sprawl is directly dependent on state intervention, and, in particular, the U.S. state.

This fact would seemingly counter the view that the U.S. state plays an ostensibly minimal/unimportant role in the operation of its domestic economy. Linda Weiss (1998), in her book entitled *The Myth of the Powerless State*, empirically demonstrates, contrary to the empirical claims of the globalization proponents, that states throughout the world shape, in important ways, their countries' relations with the global market (e.g., influencing domestic investment patterns and promoting particular industrial sectors) (also see Boyer and Drache 1996; Weiss 2003; Katzenstein 2005; Chang 2008). Nevertheless, while she holds that the United States' foreign policy is "strong," Weiss contends that the U.S. state is domestically "weak" (also see Evans 1997). She specifically holds that "America's strong focus on foreign policy and international capacity may well be a consequence of its weakness in the domestic [economic] arena" (4). When considering urban sprawl and its impact on both the U.S. economy and the world economy, what becomes evident, however, is that the U.S. state does play a key role in the operation of its domestic economy. Moreover, what also comes into relief is that U.S. foreign policy, especially as it relates to oil, is directly linked to its domestic economic policies.

What may be confusing observers such as Weiss is that U.S. domestic economic policies do not necessarily benefit its domestic economy—at least as measured in the balance of trade. (Weiss [1998], in particular, argues that a strong state is one that deploys its industrial, investment, and labor policies to improve its economy's relative performance in the global economy. She regards these policies as determining a state's transformative capacity.) So whereas most states, including those in the advanced industrialized world, intervene into the economy primarily to improve their nation's trade position, U.S. trade and domestic policies have in the long term operated to benefit the overall operation of the global economy. Thus, U.S. trade policies, coupled with pro–urban sprawl policies, along with oil policies (described below), have worked to deteriorate the U.S. trade position to the benefit of the global economy. The United States has been running a substantial and growing trade deficit for decades (Bonker 1988; Gordon 2001; Cline 2005). This deficit peaked in 2004 at more than $600 billion, in 2005 at $716 billion, and at $764 billion in 2006 (these are the largest trade deficits for any nation in modern history) (Becker 2005; Borak 2006; Goodman and Henderson 2007).

## THE U.S. STATE AND URBAN SPRAWL

It has been long understood that government policies abet the operation of the market economy (Ely 1914; Commons 1924; Coase 1960). The state provision of such infrastructure as roads, schools, ports, and courts facilitates the production and distribution of goods and services in important and central ways (Barrow 1998; Gough 2000; O'Connor 2002). In the case of the United States, the federal government, since the Progressive Era at the turn of the turn of the twentieth century, has posited regulatory regimes designed to protect the value of investments, stabilize the operation of the market, and enhance the long-term profitability of capital (Kolko 1977; Higgins-Evenson 2003). During the Great Depression in the 1930s, the U.S. federal government took an even more direct role in the economy in an effort to foster economic recovery during this period (Graham 1976; Bernstein 1987; Gordon 1994).

In the mid-1930s, in order to foster economic recovery, the federal government put forward policies to promote urban sprawl. The techniques of urban sprawl were developed by real estate interests that sought to bring utility to their land on the urban periphery (Weiss 1987; Knox 2008). The sprawling of urban America began during the late nineteenth century (chapter 3 of this book). It was at this time that the trolley, or electric streetcar, proved to be a technically and economically viable means to bring utility to land that was beyond walking distance of employment, goods, and services (Foster 1981; McShane 1994; Bruegmann 2005; Gonzalez 2005a, ch. 4). Notwithstanding the efforts of land developers to sprawl urban development through the use of the trolley, urban areas were compact and highly congested in the late nineteenth and early twentieth centuries (Rosen 1986; Schultz 1989; Fogelson 2001; Tebeau 2003; Beauregard 2006; Norton 2008). With the price of an automobile within reach of the average consumer and growing consumer confidence in cars (Flink 1975; 1990), land developers embraced the automobile as a low-cost way to increase the utility of their land—and hence its economic value. As a result, by the 1920s large-scale land developers began to shape their planned communities on the urban periphery around the automobile. This trend was particularly evident in Los Angeles (Foster 1975; Wachs 1984; Weiss 1987; Hise 1997).

As I outline in chapter 4 of this book, it was within the context of the Great Depression that the federal government came to aggressively subsidize urban sprawl. Sprawl became a means to revive the moribund U.S. economy. It specifically became a way for the economy to profitably absorb the surplus capital/savings in U.S. financial institutions. Perhaps more importantly, urban sprawl served to increase demand for the output of the U.S. industrial base. By the 1920s the United States was the world's leading producer of consumer durables, especially of automobiles. It should be noted that automotive production had broad implications for the U.S. industrial base, because by the 1920s automobile manufacturers became the leading consumers of steel, glass, and rubber. So, as described in chapter 4, when automobile consumption collapsed in the early 1930s this had reverberations throughout the manufacturing sector.

The federal government helped push urban development horizontally through a program that guaranteed home loans for newly constructed housing on the urban periphery (Jackson 1985; Weiss 1987; Hornstein 2005; Fein 2008). Such loan guarantees encouraged home construction on the urban outskirts, where homeowners would have to purchase automobiles to get around.

In the 1950s, the federal government financed an extensive highway system that helped further spur the sprawling of urban regions. Moreover, the federal government and states established what are known as highway trust funds to build and maintain highway and road systems. These trust funds are financed through earmarked gasoline taxes and other automotive fees (Burnham 1961; Rose 1979; Whitt 1982; Kay 1998; Gutfreund 2004; Baum-Snow 2005; Rose, Seely, and Barrett 2006).

U.S. foreign policy is also directly involved in the sprawling of urban development in the United States. Urban sprawl is predicated on superabundant supplies of oil. Ample supplies of petroleum mean that the price of gasoline/diesel will remain relatively low, and this facilitates the long driving distances inherent in sprawled urban development. From the late nineteenth century until the middle of the twentieth century, the United States was the world's leading producer of oil. The U.S. firm Standard Oil was the first to globalize the trade in petroleum products—in particular kerosene, used for indoor lighting. This trade was initially based on Pennsylvania oil production. Later oil finds in the states of California, Oklahoma, Texas, Indiana, and Louisiana established the United States as the world's prime source of oil until the 1950s (Franks and Lambert 1982; Yergin 1991; Davis 1993, ch. 3; Black 2000; Olien and Olien 2002; Sabin 2004).

Improved refining techniques allowed more oil to be refined into gasoline for internal combustion engines, just as the electric light bulb had severely curtailed the kerosene market at the turn of the century. The abundant supply of oil, and hence gasoline, spurred automobile development, production, and consumption in the United States (Flink 1975; 1990; Thomas 1977; Bardou et al. 1982, ch. 6; Barker 1985; St. Clair 1986; Podobnik 2006).

While large domestic supplies of oil spurred the automobile trade and facilitated the urban development policies of the federal government, the inability of U.S. petroleum production to increase with the growing demand for gasoline portended severe limitations for the urban sprawl model of economic growth. As early as the 1920s, U.S. oil firms were concerned that domestic supplies could not meet the demand resulting from expanding automobile usage. The U.S. government responded by successfully negotiating, with France and Great Britain, access for U.S. firms to oil supplies within modern-day Iraq (Yergin 1991; Randall 2005). So even during this early period of automobile use, U.S. policy was designed to expand oil supply in response to growing demand, and not an effort to curtail demand to remain within the confines of otherwise abundant U.S. oil supplies. During the post–World War II period, when urban sprawl became central to maintaining U.S./world economic stability, oil became a vital economic resource. As explained in chapter 5, by 1973 U.S. foreign policy became especially geared toward maintaining an ample flow of oil from the Persian Gulf region. The countries of the Persian Gulf hold the majority of known oil reserves.

Whereas U.S. policies promoted low-density urban development, in Europe public policies served to keep urban areas relatively compact. In the 1920s Western and Central Europe did not possess the economic factors that would have made urban sprawl immediately profitable. It did not have much surplus capital to invest in new housing stock—indeed, during this period most of these countries were deeply in debt to U.S. financiers. Also, unlike the U.S. economy, the advanced economies of Europe were not geared toward the production of consumer durables (Fearon 1987; Atkinson 2004).

It should also be noted that the politics surrounding transportation and land use were decidedly different in Europe than in the United States. As outlined in chapter 3 of this book, in the United States the trolley was largely deployed to inflate land values on the urban periphery by rendering such land usable as suburban housing. The utilization of trolley systems in the United States to inflate land values served to undermine the economic and political viability of U.S. trolley systems, as these systems were configured in an economically and geographically inefficient manner (Dewees 1970; Foster 1981). In Europe, in contrast, the trolley was used predominately to bring economically efficient transportation to urban zones. As a result, in Europe the advent of the trolley did not push urban regions in a horizontal direction, as it did in the United States (McKay 1976; 1988; Dunn 1981; Yago 1984). In most U.S. cities comprehensive rail systems do not exist today, whereas in Europe almost every town with a substantial population has a fixed rail transport network (Banister et al. 2000; Beatley 2000; Sheehan 2001, 48).

These factors help explain why European countries did not enact policies to promote urban sprawl during the 1930s and during the post–World War II period. They do not necessarily explain, however, why these countries have generally adopted policies that curb horizontal urban development. The predominant explanation for this can be found in energy politics. Unlike the United States, for most of their history the advanced economies of Western and Central Europe did not have much appreciable domestic oil production. Also, whereas the United States had massive supplies of coal and natural gas (Schurr and Netschert 1960; Vietor 1980; Sanders 1981; Banks 1995; Adams 2006), Europe did not (Maull 1980; Hatch 1986; Holter 1992; Haugland, Bergensen, and Roland 1998). Such ample supplies of fossil fuels can be used to cheaply electrify, as well as heat and cool, large homes on the urban periphery. Energy expert Paul Roberts (2004) explains that contemporary U.S. households are "at least twice as energy-intensive as European and Japanese households" (152;

also see International Energy Agency 1997, 162; Fackler 2007; Roberts 2008). Finally, in the post–World War II era, the countries of Europe did not have the military and political capacity to intervene in the Middle East to ensure that the oil from this region amply flowed.

Thus, the policies historically employed throughout the leading countries of Europe that serve as barriers to urban sprawl can be viewed as efforts to minimize the risk to these countries' economies posed by their tenuous access to the key global sources of fossil fuels. (For a further discussion of this see chapter 5.) The policies in question include steep gasoline and energy taxes (Lucas 1985; Haugland, Bergensen, and Roland 1998; Nivola 1999; Sheehan 2001, 48; Romero 2005). Significantly, these taxes are not earmarked for road or highway development, as occurs in the United States, but instead go into general revenue funds (Dunn 1981, ch. 7; Nivola and Crandall 1995). Governments in Western and Central Europe also tend to coordinate mass transit and urban development (Beatley 2000). By way of contrast, in the United States there is rarely such coordination and planning (Warner and Molotch 2000; Sheehan 2001, 42–47; Gotham 2002; Portney 2003; Dilworth 2005).

Thanks to radically divergent energy, transportation, and land use policies, Europe and the United States have dramatically different urban landscapes. These differences are all the more significant because the two regions are not that different geographically and possess similar demographic characteristics. For instance, whereas Belgium and the state of New Jersey have a similar land to population ratio and per capita income, per capita automobile ownership and use is substantially higher in New Jersey (Kenworthy and Laube 1999; Nivola 1999).

In general, the United States has the most sprawled urban regions in the world. This is documented in Kenworthy and Laube's *An International Sourcebook of Automobile Dependence in Cities 1960–1990*, published in 1999. Two key indicators of sprawl and automobile dependency are per capita automobile ownership and automobile usage. In Kenworthy and Laube's study of forty-six international cities they found that the U.S. cities studied had the highest total figures on both counts. (These cities are listed in Table 1.1.) The authors group the cities they studied into six countries/regions: (1) U.S. cities, (2) Australian cities, (3) Canadian cities, (4) European cities, (5) wealthy Asian cities, and (6) developing Asian cities. The U.S. cities in Kenworthy and Laube's analysis were Boston, Chicago, Denver, Detroit, Houston, Los Angeles, New York, Phoenix, Portland, Sacramento, San Diego, San Francisco, and Washington. The Australian cities were as follows: Adelaide, Brisbane, Canberra, Melbourne, Perth, and Sydney. The Canadian cities were: Calgary, Edmonton, Montreal, Ottawa, Toronto, Vancouver, and Winnipeg. European cities: Amsterdam, Brussels, Copenhagen, Frankfurt, Hamburg,

Table 1.1. The 46 Cities of Kenworthy and Laube's (1999) Study

| U.S. cities | Australian cities | Canadian cities | European cities | Wealthy Asian cities | Developing Asian cities |
|---|---|---|---|---|---|
| Boston | Adelaide | Calgary | Amsterdam | Hong Kong | Bangkok |
| Chicago | Brisbane | Edmonton | Brussels | Singapore | Jakarta |
| Denver | Canberra | Montreal | Copenhagen | Tokyo | Kuala Lumpur |
| Detroit | Melbourne | Ottawa | Frankfurt | | Manila |
| Houston | Perth | Toronto | Hamburg | | Seoul |
| Los Angeles | Sydney | Vancouver | London | | Surabaya |
| New York | | Winnipeg | Munich | | |
| Phoenix | | | Paris | | |
| Portland | | | Stockholm | | |
| Sacramento | | | Vienna | | |
| San Diego | | | Zürich | | |
| San Francisco | | | | | |
| Washington, D.C. | | | | | |

London, Munich, Paris, Stockholm, Vienna, and Zurich. Wealthy Asian cities: Hong Kong, Singapore, and Tokyo. Developing Asian cities: Bangkok, Jakarta, Kuala Lumpur, Manila, Seoul, and Surabaya. As shown in Table 1.2, in the U.S. cities, in 1990 there were 604 automobiles per one thousand people. In the other cities the number of automobiles per thousand individuals were as follows: Australian cities, 491; Canadian, 524; European, 392; wealthy Asian, 123; and developing Asian, 102 (529).

In 1990 each automobile in those U.S. cities studied was driven an average of 11,155 kilometers. In Australia this average was 6,571; Canada, 6,551; Europe, 4,519; wealthy Asian cities, 1,487; and developing Asian cities, 1848 (529). The ratio of the average use of each automobile in the U.S. cities compared to the others was: Australia, 1.70; Canada, 1.70; Europe, 2.47; wealthy Asian cities, 7.50; and developing Asian cities, 6.04 (530). The wide gap between automobile use in the United States and everywhere else prompted Kenworthy and Laube to note that "vehicle use not ownership is the primary factor in determining outcomes such as congestion, fuel use and emissions." They go on to assert that "if cities build in compulsory car use through low-density, heavily zoned land uses which make travel distances long and the use of other modes very difficult, then high car use is almost assured" (530).[6]

With much of the economic growth in the United States throughout the 1990s occurring in the southern and southwestern regions of the country (Abbott 1987; Dreier, Mollenkopf, and Swanstrom 2001; Pack 2005), the average commuting distance between home and work, and the average amount of automobile use, has increased (Lopez and Hynes 2003). The southern and southwestern urban regions of the United States are highly sprawled and automobile dependent (Nivola 1999; Bento et al. 2005; Kahn 2006). For instance, in Los Angeles, located in the southwest, the average distance between home and work was 17.8 kilometers in 1990, while in Houston (the south) it was 19.1. In Los Angeles, during 1990, the percentage of people riding public transportation to work was 6.7. In Phoenix (the southwest) and Houston that figure was 2.1 and 4.1 percent, respectively. By way of comparison, New York City, in the northeast, in 1990 had an average distance to work of 13.6 kilometers, whereas in Boston (the northeast) it was 10.1. In New York the percentage of people using public transportation to get to work was 26 percent in 1990. Among residents of Boston 14.7 percent took public transportation to work in that year (Kenworthy and Laube 1999, 610; also see Kahn 2006, 115 and 117).

Table 1.2. Comparative Urban Automobile Use*

| Region | Automobile Ownership (per 1000 people) | Average Automobile Use (kilometers) | Ratio of Average U.S. Automobile Use Compared to Other Urban Areas |
|---|---|---|---|
| U.S. cities | 604 | 11155 | —— |
| Australian cities | 491 | 6571 | 1.70 |
| Canadian cities | 524 | 6551 | 1.70 |
| European cities | 392 | 4519 | 2.47 |
| Wealthy Asian cities | 123 | 1487 | 7.50 |
| Developing Asian cities | 102 | 1848 | 6.04 |

*Source:* Kenworthy and Laub (1999), 529–30
*Figures for most recent year available: 1990

Table 1.3. Carbon Dioxide ($CO_2$) Emissions Per $1 million of GDP of Selected Countries*

| Countries | Emissions (in tons) of $CO_2$ per $1 million of GDP |
|---|---|
| France | 56 |
| Japan | 57 |
| Germany | 80 |
| South Korea | 84 |
| United Kingdom | 118 |
| United States | 171 |
| India | 621 |
| China | 731 |
| Russia | 914 |

*Source:* Environmental Performance Index (2006)
*All figures are for 2004.[7] All countries selected have populations over 45 million

The United States' relatively energy-intense urban transportation system at least partially accounts for the fact that, according to an international study produced by Yale and Columbia universities, every $1 million of the U.S. GDP resulted in 171 tons of carbon dioxide emissions in 2004.[8] As outlined in table 1.3, this is three times the rate of the advanced economies of France (56) and Japan (57). It is more than twice the emission rate of Germany (80) and South Korea (84) per $1 million of GDP. The United Kingdom was found to have a rate of 118 tons per $1 million of GDP (Barringer 2006 Jan. 23; *Environmental Performance Index* 2006).

The United States' heavy use of the automobile, coupled with its energy-intensive housing stock, helps explain the per capita carbon dioxide emissions data recently released by the International Energy Agency (Table 1.4). The United States emitted 19.6 tons of carbon dioxide for every one of its residents in 2005, while France emitted 6.2 tons; United Kingdom 8.8; South Korea 9.3; Japan 9.5; and Germany 9.9. Even the highly energy inefficient economies of India, China, and Russia emitted significantly less anthropogenic carbon dioxide than the United States on a per capita basis in 2005, 1.05, 3.9, and 10.8, respectively (International Energy Agency 2007, Part Two, 49–51) (The Russian economy emitted 914 tons of $CO_2$ for every $1 million of GDP, while China emitted 731 and India 621, respectively [*Environmental Performance Index* 2006]).

Table 1.4. Carbon Dioxide ($CO_2$) Per Capita Emissions of Selected Countries*

| Countries | Per Capita $CO_2$ Emissions (in tons) |
|---|---|
| United States | 19.6 |
| Russia | 10.8 |
| Germany | 9.9 |
| Japan | 9.5 |
| South Korea | 9.3 |
| United Kingdom | 8.8 |
| France | 6.2 |
| China | 3.9 |
| India | 1.05 |

Source: International Energy Agency 2007, Part Two, 49–51
*All figures are for 2005. All countries selected have populations over 45 million

## OVERVIEW OF BOOK

There is a debate among scholars over the role of the state in the operation of the global economy. The most prominent view of the state within the global economy is that it is becoming increasingly irrelevant, as the unfettered market has apparently become the preeminent world economic force. With the state receding as a global economic factor, political power has ostensibly shifted to such international institutions as the World Bank, the International Monetary Fund, and the World Trade Organization, as well as to those who make decisions within major transnational corporations (i.e., TCC).

Drawing heavily on traditional Marxist thought, Ellen Meiksins Wood holds that the state in the global economy is central to its operation and maintenance. Wood explains that it is instrumental in upholding the capitalist world order. Additionally, the U.S. state is particularly important in stimulating world economic demand. The fostering of sprawled urban regions by the U.S. government can be viewed as a specific and important effort to increase worldwide consumption and ultimately stabilize the global economy. Historically, sprawl was embraced as a means to increase demand for consumer durables during the Great Depression. The post–World War II boom in U.S. consumption of consumer durables (Olney 1991; French 1997; Brenner 2002) can be directly linked to urban sprawl and the public policies that promoted such sprawl (Beauregard 2006). In the contemporary period, the U.S. state plays the central role in spurring urban sprawl. It does so through a foreign policy that seeks to guarantee the flow of Middle East oil, through cheap credit policies ("Greenspan Defends Homeowner Debt Levels" 2004; Gotham 2006), land use policies that dictate the building of single-family homes, and an aggressive road and highway building program. These policies and the urban sprawl they foster can help explain why the United States is the largest consumer in the world, and also has a very low savings rate (Goodman 2008 Feb 5; Wilcox 2008). American families spend money on multiple automobiles so members can get to and fro, on furniture and appliances to fill relatively large homes, and on energy expenses to power their vehicles, appliances, and to heat and cool their relatively spacious abodes.

While urban sprawl in the United States serves to prop up the world economy, urban sprawl has a number of environmental costs associated with it. Firstly, horizontal urban expansion destroys open space and wilderness (Hayden 2003; Johnson and Klemens 2005; Schipper 2008). Urban sprawl also draws down finite fossil fuels at a prodigious rate (Goodstein 2004; Roberts 2004; Podobnik 2006). This huge use of fossil fuels substantially contributes to the climate change phenomenon. These fuels are being consumed at such high rates that the carbon dioxide emitted by their burning cannot be benignly absorbed by the biosphere of the planet (Clark and York 2005; Volk 2008).

How did the policies underlying the creation of the sprawled urban zones in the United States come into being? Economic elite theory offers the deepest insight in the development of the sprawled urban zones of the United States. This theory posits that economic elites and producer groups are at the center of public policymaking. This theory, along with competing theories of the public policymaking process, is laid out in chapter 2. I outline in chapter 3 how the techniques of urban sprawl were developed by landed interests and land developers (i.e., producer groups) who sought to enhance the economic utility of their landholdings. More importantly, sprawl was embraced by economic elites in the 1930s as the means to address the economic exigency of the Great Depression (chapter 4). In chapter 5 I describe how U.S. oil policy was shaped by economic elites. In chapter 6 I outline how the response of business groups, as well as environmental groups, to climate change has not been to directly address urban sprawl but to advocate the creation and deployment of technologies (including alternative energy) that would abate the emission of greenhouse gases and allow urban sprawl to continue and expand.

# Chapter Two

# Political Economy and the Imperatives of the State

In the preceding chapter, I outlined how urban sprawl beginning in the 1930s served as a means to revive the economy, and, more specifically, to absorb the United States' surplus capital and the output of its productive capacity. My argument, however, is not limited to an analysis of the political economy of urban sprawl.[1] Of equal importance here is the identification of the political processes that over history have prompted urban sprawl in the United States. Thus, while public policies that promote urban sprawl economically benefit real estate interests, lending institutions, and industrial producers (especially automobile makers), did other actors nevertheless politically prompt the sprawling of urban America?

To answer this question in this chapter I survey the literature on policymaking in the U.S. Pluralism became the predominant view of political power and policymaking in the immediate post–World War II period. In the aftermath of the social movements of the 1960s and 1970s skepticism spread about the pluralists' assertions about the distribution of political influence and the putatively permeable and inclusive nature of the public policymaking process in the United States. In this context a new view of the policymaking process as shaped by entrenched special interests came into prominence. This view is entitled plural elitism. The social movements of the 1960s and 1970s, in addition to modifying the understanding of political power in the United States, also sparked the activation of numerous public interest groups and activists seeking to challenge the position of otherwise dominant special interests. This has prompted some political scientists to hold that special interest dominance in Washington, D.C., has been transformed into issue networks, whereby public interest organizations and activists vie with influential interest groups over the formation of public policy. Among these public organizations and activists are environmentalists.

19

Despite the challenge of the environmental social movement of the late 1960s and early 1970s, and the oil crises of the 1970s as well as, more recently, the apparent perils of climate change, the U.S. government has maintained its commitment to urban sprawl. This would strongly indicate that urban sprawl in the United States is not the result of special interest politics, but more likely an objective or "imperative" of the state. Two competing approaches seek to explain who determines the imperatives of the state and how they are met: state autonomy theory and economic elite theory.

I begin this chapter by examining plural elitism and the advent of issue networks. Next I discuss the idea of imperatives of the state and the two competing approaches that seek to explain how these imperatives are determined.

I conclude the chapter with an overview of how economic elites in the United States have historically sought to address airborne pollution. This overview is drawn from my 2005 book, *The Politics of Air Pollution*. As is evident from this overview, economic elites in the United States have tried to reduce localized air pollution through the development and deployment of technology. In chapter 6 I outline how the international business community currently seeks to deal with climate change also through the development and deployment of technology.

## PLURALISM ELITISM

Pluralism arose as the dominant political science paradigm in the post–World War II period. Early proponents of pluralism minimized/obscured the political hegemony that big business and big labor exercised under the auspices of the New Deal (Manley 1983; Lindblom 1977, 1982, 1983, 1988). Pluralist theorists, most prominent among them being Robert Dahl (Dahl and Lindblom 1953; Dahl 1956, 1961 [2005]; Connolly 2005), held that various interest groups, including major corporations and labor unions, would exercise influence over government. E. E. Schnattschneider, writing in 1960, aptly described, however, the numerical preponderance of business related groups in Washington, D.C. (20–36), and stated that *"even non-business [lobbying] organizations reflect an upper-class tendency"* (33; emphasis in original). Thus, while pluralists in the postwar period were promoting the idea of an inclusive and permeable public policymaking process, the reality was a policymaking process limited to a relatively narrow grouping of elites, including members of the upper class pushing their specific projects (Mills 1956; Domhoff 1967). Among these projects would be the setting aside for preservation certain areas of wilderness that were deemed to have scenic and/or scientific value (Schrepfer 1983, 2005; Gonzalez 2001a, ch. 3 and 4; M. Harvey 2005).

The reality of the configuration of political power in New Deal America was not widely acknowledged/realized until the social movements of the 1960s and early 1970s besieged U.S. political institutions (e.g., the antiwar movement, the civil rights movement, and the environmental movement). What came into full relief during this period was that government was not a neutral arena whereby different interest groups brought their political resources to bear (i.e., money, votes, prestige) as held by early pluralist thinkers. Nor was the successful mobilization of interest groups all that was needed to influence/shape the policymaking process (Truman 1951). Instead, political influence in the United States came to be viewed as consistent with plural elitism.

Plural elitism theorists hold that certain interests are entrenched and exercise dominant influence over policy formation. Theodore Lowi (1979) explains that the allocation of policymaking authority to specific agencies within the executive branch leads to the "capture" of those agencies by special interests—and thus the establishment of what he calls "subgovernments." The philosophy/practice of ceding policymaking authority to executive branch agencies is named by Lowi "interest-group liberalism."

Grant McConnell (1966), like Lowi, attributed the diffusion of state power to a dominant political philosophy. This political philosophy, according to McConnell, is rooted in discourses developed during the Progressive Era. These discourses posit that democracy is most effectively applied in small bureaucratic units. In turn, this fracturing of the federal government into a multitude of small units allows the capture of significant amounts of state power by special interests. Hence, while both McConnell and Lowi trace the public philosophy that has predicated the creation of a governmental structure that promotes capture by special interests to different philosophical precepts, both their conclusions are similar.

While Lowi and McConnell attribute the creation of subgovernments to the institutional structure of the federal government, especially the executive branch, and the legislative practice of delegating policymaking authority to executive branch agencies, Dahl and Lindblom (1976), in a modification of early pluralist thought, argue that business groups in particular are going to have privileged access over the policymaking process. Subgovernments, they aver, are less the result of happenstance and more the result of the fact that businesspeople are directly responsible for running the economy. The result of this responsibility is the "privileged participation of business" in government:

Businessmen are not ordered by law to perform the many organizational and leadership tasks that are delegated to them. All these societies operate by rules that require that businessmen be induced rather than commanded. It is therefore clear that these societies must provide sufficient benefits or indulgences to businessmen to constitute an inducement for them to perform their assigned tasks.

The consequence of these arrangements—peculiar as they would appear to a man from Mars—is that it becomes a major task of government to design and maintain an inducement system for businessmen, to be solicitous of business interests, and to grant to them, for its value as an incentive, an intimacy of participation in government itself. In all these respects the relation between government and business is unlike the relation between government and any other group in the society. (Dahl and Lindblom 1976, xxxvii)

Therefore, subgovernments are the logical outcome of an economic system that relies on private elites to deliver economic prosperity. By giving businesspeople dominant influence over those government agencies that shape the behavior of the economy, this helps to ensure that the policies of these agencies will lead to economic growth and stability. Miller (1976) refers to this arrangement as the "fusion of economic and political power."

Dahl and Lindblom's argument that political authority over economic policies must be ceded to economic interests in order for those policies to be successful is consistent with the history of Federal Housing Authority (FHA). As outlined in chapter 4, the FHA was given responsibility over the federal government's prime housing program beginning the 1930s, and policymaking positions within the FHA were granted to prominent individuals from the housing industry as well as from the financial sector. As indicated by Dahl and Lindblom, the fact that individuals with such backgrounds were given responsibility to set the federal government's housing policy is logical since it was the housing industry and the financial sector that were ultimately entrusted with building and financing the nation's housing, even that housing that was sponsored by the FHA. From the mid-1930s into the late 1960s the FHA played the key governmental role in subsidizing and encouraging urban sprawl in the United States.

## ISSUE NETWORKS

The social movements of the 1960s and the early 1970s did initiate the expansion of the number of public interest organizations, and the activation of public interest advocates (Walker 1983, 1991, ch. 4; Baumgartner and Leech 1998, 103). During this period, environmental groups, in particular, increased significantly in number, membership, and staff (Baumgartner and Jones 1993, 187; Lowry 1998, 47; Shaiko 1999; Rose 2000; Jones and

Baumgartner 2005). These newly created groups, and advocates, have been participating in such issue and policy areas as the environment, health care, consumer affairs, race relations, good government, and poverty (for examples see Heinz et al. 1993; Kraft and Kamieniecki 2007). It is these public interest advocates and groups that Hugh Heclo (1978) views as the primary challenge to the relationship between special interests and subgovernments as described by Lowi, McConnell, and Dahl and Lindblom. With the introduction of these actors, the relationship between government agencies and interest groups has been transformed from capture to one of issue networks. Heclo argues:

> It would be foolish to suggest that the clouds of issue networks that have accompanied expanding national policies are set to replace the more familiar politics of subgovernments in Washington. What they are doing is to overlay the once stable political reference points with new forces that complicate calculations, decrease predictability, and impose considerable strains on those charged with government leadership. The overlay of networks and issue politics not only confronts but also seeps down into the formerly well-established politics of particular policies and programs. (1978, 105)

Therefore, with the expansion of federal programs into new areas, such as air pollution, medical care for the poor, urban renewal, and civil rights, public interest organizations and individuals have entered into the policy fray, thus challenging the near-monopoly on information, perspective, and other political resources (e.g., electoral votes) held by heretofore unchallenged special interests.

Heclo points to energy policy during the Carter administration as an example of what he feels is the result of expanding and increasingly complex issue networks. He argues that

> the debate on energy policy is rich in examples of the kaleidoscopic interaction of changing issue networks. The Carter administration's initial proposal was worked out among experts who were closely tied in to conservation-minded networks. Soon it became clear that those concerned with macroeconomic policies had been largely bypassed in the planning, and last-minute amendments were made in the proposal presented to Congress, a fact that was not lost on the networks of leading economists and economic correspondents. Once congressional consideration began, it quickly became evident that attempts to define the energy debate in terms of a classic confrontation between big

oil companies and consumer interest were doomed. More and more policy watchers joined in the debate, bringing to it their own concerns and analyses: tax reformers, nuclear power specialists, civil rights groups interested in more jobs; the list soon grew beyond the wildest dreams of the original energy policy planners. (1978, 104)

Therefore, these issue networks have in a significant sense remedied the classic Schnattschneider (1960) dilemma. Namely, issue networks have, according to Heclo and others (e.g., Bosso 1987, 2005; Baumgartner and Leech 1998, 111–14; Sabatier 1999; Duffy 2003), successfully expanded the "scope of conflict." Now broader public interests are generally incorporated into policy deliberations. Andrew McFarland (2004, 2007) labels this new interest group milieu neopluralism (also see Grossman and Helpman 2001; Kamieniecki 2006; Yackee and Yackee 2006).

In spite of the activation of numerous public interest groups and activists, including ones active on the question of air pollution (Marzotto, Burnor, and Bonham 2000; Gonzalez 2005a, ch. 6), land use (Bullard and Johnson 1997; Hayden 2003), energy (Hess 2007), and more recently climate change (chapter 6 of this book), the government's pro-urban sprawl policies continue. This would indicate that urban sprawl in the United States is not solely the result of real estate and financial interests successfully pushing their specific and narrow agendas. Instead, urban sprawl appears to be an imperative of the state. The question is, Who has set this imperative?

## IMPERATIVES OF THE STATE

Political theorist John Dryzek (1996a) argues in his critique of traditional pluralism that "irrespective of what interest groups seek, states must meet certain imperatives" within capitalist societies (478). Hence, as Dryzek explains, pluralism fails as a policymaking model because it does not orient the researcher to the operation of capitalism and how it creates certain imperatives for the state. Following neo-Marxist views of the state and politics (Poulantzas 1973; Barrow 1993, ch. 2; Aronowitz and Bratsis 2002; O'Connor 2002; Wetherly 2005), Dryzek (1996b) holds that these imperatives are forwarding the private accumulation of capital (i.e., maintaining a strong economy) and maintaining the legitimacy of the state within the context of a market economy. Also emphasizing the role of political elites in setting the imperatives of the state and how they are met are the proponents of state autonomy theory. A second explanation of who determines the imperatives of the state looks to economic elites.

## STATE AUTONOMY THEORY

At the core of state autonomy theory is the notion that officials within the state can and do behave autonomously of all social groups.[2] Officials within the state have special theoretical significance because they are often called upon to deal with political and economic matters. Moreover, they are also provided in many instances with the resources, such as legal authority and a budget, to do so (Poulantzas 1973; Nordlinger 1981; Skowronek 1982; Skocpol 1985; Finegold and Skocpol 1995; Klyza 1996; Carpenter 2001; Aronowitz and Bratsis 2002; O'Connor 2002; Wetherly 2005). Indicative of the argument that autonomous officials within the government drive state behavior, Adam Rome (2001), in his book linking the rise of modern environmentalism in the United States to urban sprawl, holds that the federal government, beginning in the 1920s, viewed low-density housing development as the means to attain broad-based home ownership (ch. 1) (also see Radford 1996). Also consistent with the state autonomy position is Stephen Krasner's (1979) argument that U.S. foreign policy as it relates to raw materials, including petroleum, has historically been shaped by the ideology of officials within the state.

In this context, autonomous policymakers can and do draw upon different members of any given issue network to determine how to prioritize various imperatives and how to address them (Skocpol 1992; Skocpol, Ganz, and Munson 2000). In this way, public interest advocates are incorporated into the policymaking process. Scientists and experts have specific importance within state autonomy theory. This is because they offer the technical know-how to instruct public officials. Scientists and experts also orient state officials to the political, economic, environmental, and social issues that must be addressed in order to avoid more serious difficulties (Mcgrath 2002; Rich 2004; Layzer 2007). According to Theda Skocpol (1986/87), the legitimacy and usefulness of experts is enhanced by the fact that they "most often . . . attempt to act as 'third-force' mediators, downplaying the role of class interests and class struggles and promoting the expansion of state or other 'public' capacities to regulate the economy and social relations" (332).

On the question of climate change, however, the federal government has shunned the advice and activism of numerous scientists and environmental groups (Shulman 2006; Heilprin 2007; Gautier 2008). A strong consensus has developed among scientists that the continuing uncontrolled emission of carbon dioxide holds seemingly dire consequences for the earth's biosphere. This consensus includes the International Panel on Climate Change, a panel composed of leading climate scientists (Houghton 2004; Gautier and Fellous 2008). The Clinton administration did sign the 1997 Kyoto Protocol, which is geared toward abating greenhouse gases. Nevertheless, it did so reluctantly and the administration demanded a number of loopholes for the United States in the implementation of the protocol. As a result of U.S. efforts to gain exemptions for itself in the application of the protocol, an agreement to implement the protocol could not be negotiated. In early 2001 the second Bush administration withdrew from the protocol (Brown 2002; Lisowski 2002; Fisher 2004, ch. 6; Cass 2006; Nordhaus 2008). With the United States withdrawn from the protocol, a sufficient number of the remaining signatories successfully negotiated its implementation, and among these countries the protocol went into effect in 2005.

The protocol initially called upon the United States to reduce all greenhouse gas emissions, including that of carbon dioxide, 7 percent below 1990 emission levels by 2012; the European Union countries by 8 percent; and Japan 6 percent. Overall, industrialized countries were to reduce their carbon dioxide emissions by an average of 5 percent from 1990 levels by 2012.

In 1998 the Energy Information Administration (EIA) released a report predicting the economic costs for the United States associated with meeting its Kyoto Protocol target. The EIA describes itself as an "independent statistical and analytical agency in the U.S. Department of Energy" (EIA 1998, title page). According to this report, in order to meet the Kyoto Protocol target, coal consumption in the United States would have to drop between 18 and 77 percent from current projected rates by 2010 (EIA 1998, xviii), and petroleum use would have to be reduced between 2 and 13 percent (EIA 1998, xix). The upper range of reductions represents a projection based on the assumption that the total reduction in the emission of greenhouse gases stipulated in the protocol would be completely absorbed by the U.S. economy. The lower range represents a 24 percent carbon dioxide emission level above the 1990 emission level, and it assumes credits for sinks (e.g., forests) and international activities (such as trading of carbon emission permits), but with some direct domestic actions to reduce climate change emissions. The upper limit range represents a 542 million metric ton annual reduction in carbon dioxide emissions from the U.S. economy between 2008 and 2012, whereas the lower range would represent an annual reduction of approximately 122 million metric tons. Both of these figures are compared to no regulatory action being taken (EIA 1998, xii–xiii).

Therefore, the Kyoto Protocol represented the potential of significantly increasing energy costs in the United States. As a result, the protocol would have created substantial disincentives for urban sprawl in the United States. According to the EIA report, electricity prices would increase from 20 to 86 percent in 2010 if the Kyoto Protocol were implemented by the United States (EIA 1998, xv), and "the average price" of gasoline would be between 11 and 53 percent higher (EIA 1998, xviii). Given that the European Union as a whole and Japan have more compact cities and emit less carbon dioxide per capita than the United States, their costs associated with reducing carbon dioxide emissions are substantially lower than those of the United States (Cline 1992; Nordhaus and Boyer 2000; Uzawa 2003).

Such price increases would undermine demand for spacious housing on the urban periphery, and in turn create incentives for more compact communities with smaller housing units and greater opportunities for inexpensive mass rapid transportation (streetcars, subways, buses) (Bulkeley and Betsill 2003). Denser urban areas, with smaller living quarters, would lessen demand for land, automobiles, electricity, gasoline, appliances, and furniture. Particularly significant for the automobile industry, densely organized communities, coupled with increased fuel costs, would push consumers away from larger and more profitable vehicles (e.g., light trucks), which are substantially less fuel efficient than smaller, less profitable vehicles (Bradsher 2002; Ford 2004; Hakim 2005 May 21).

## ECONOMIC ELITE THEORY

While plural elite theorists describe how individual corporate decision makers dominate specific and narrow policy areas (Manley 1983), economic elite theorists contend that these corporate decision makers, along with other individuals of wealth, develop and impose broadly construed policies on the state. Additionally, while plural elite theory views the business community as socially and politically fragmented, proponents of the economic elite approach hold that the owners and leadership of this community can be most aptly characterized as composing a coherent social and political unit or class (Miliband 1969; Hay, Lister, and Marsh 2006, ch. 2; Wetherly et al. 2008).

Clyde Barrow (1993) points out that "typically, members of the capitalist class [or the economic elite] are identified as those persons who manage [major] corporations and/or own those corporations." He adds that this group composes no more than 0.5 to 1.0 percent of the total U.S. population (17).[3] This group as a whole is the upper class and the upper echelon of the corporate or business community. The resource that members of the economic elite possess that allows them to exercise a high level of influence over government institutions is wealth. The wealth and income of the economic elite allow it to accumulate superior amounts of other valuable resources, such as social status, deference, prestige, organization, campaign finance, lobbying, political access, and legal and scientific expertise (Barrow 1993, 16; West and Loomis 1999; Hohenstein 2008).

Within the economic elite approach, despite the segmentation of the economic elite along lines that are related to their material holdings, most policy differences that arise due to differences in economic interests can and are mediated. There are social and organizational mechanisms that exist that allow business leaders to resolve difficulties that develop within a particular segment and between different segments of the corporate community. For specific industries, or for disagreements between different industries, trade or business associations can serve as organizations to mediate corporate conflict. Social institutions, such as social and country clubs, can also serve as means through which to develop political consensus among the upper echelon of the business community on various economic, political, and social issues (Domhoff 1974). Michael Useem (1984), based on his extensive study of large American and British corporations, argues that corporate directors who hold membership on more than one board of directors tend to serve as a means through which the corporate community achieves consensus on various political issues (also see Mintz and Schwartz 1985).

On broad issues, such as global warming, business leaders are also able to arrive at policy agreement and consensus through "policy-planning networks." According to G. William Domhoff, the policy-planning network is composed of four major components: policy discussion groups, foundations, think tanks, and university research institutes. This network's budget, in large part, is drawn directly from the corporate community (Weidenbaum 2009). Furthermore, many of the directors and trustees of the organizations that comprise this policy-planning network are often drawn directly from the upper echelons of the corporate community and from the upper class. These trustees and directors, in turn, help set the general direction of the policy-planning organizations, as well as directly choose the individuals that manage the day-to-day operation of these organizations (Domhoff 2005, ch. 4).

Domhoff describes the political behavior of those members of the economic elite that manage and operate within the policy-planning network:

> The policy-formation process is the means by which the power elite formulates policy on larger issues. It is within the organizations of the policy-planning network that the various special interests join together to forge, however, slowly and gropingly, the general policies that will benefit them as a whole. It is within the policy process that the various sectors of the business community transcend their interest-group consciousness and develop an overall class consciousness. (Domhoff 1978a, 61)

Therefore, those members of the economic elite that operate within the policy-planning network take on a broad perspective, and act on behalf of the economic elite as a whole. Within this policy-planning network members of the economic elite take general positions on such issues as foreign policy, economic policy, business regulation, environmental policy, and defense policy questions (Weinstein 1968; Eakins 1969, 1972; Kolko

1977; Domhoff 1978a, ch. 4, 2005, ch. 4; Barrow 1993, ch. 1; Gonzalez 2001a, 2001b, 2005a, 2005b).

This broad perspective also allows the policy-planning network to develop plans and positions to deal with other groups and classes. The network, for example, develops positions and plans concerning such policy areas as welfare and education. These plans can take several forms depending on the scope and level of the problems facing the business community and the state (Weinstein 1968; Eakins 1972; Domhoff 1978a, 1990, 1996, 2005; Berman 1983; Barrow 1990, 1992, 1993, ch. 1; Dowie 2001; Cyphers 2002; Parmar 2002a; Roelofs 2003).

Domhoff argues that the focal point in the policy-planning network is the policy discussion group. The other components of the policy-planning network—foundations, think tanks, and university research institutes—generally provide original research, policy specialists, and ideas to the policy discussion groups (Domhoff 1978a, 63). Policy discussion groups are largely composed of members from the corporate community and the upper class. Examples of policy discussion groups are the Business Roundtable, the Committee for Economic Development, the National Association of Manufacturers, and the U.S. Chamber of Commerce. Overall, policy discussion groups are the arenas where members of the economic elite come together with policy specialists to formulate policy positions, and where members of the economic elite evaluate policy specialists for possible service in government (Eakins 1972; Domhoff 1978a, 61–87, 2005, ch. 4; Barrow 1993, ch. 1).[4] One example of a policy discussion group is the Clean Air Working Group. It was organized by the corporate community in the 1980s and focuses on the issue of federal clean air regulations (Gonzalez 2001a, ch. 6). Additionally, as is explained in chapter 4, the outlines of U.S. foreign policy during the cold war were shaped in the Council on Foreign Relations, an economic elite–led policy discussion group.

Certain environmental groups, in terms of their leadership and/or financing, have the characteristics of economic elite–led policy-planning organizations. These groups include the Sierra Club prior to the 1960s, the Save-the-Redwoods League, and Environmental Defense. Environmental Defense, for instance, receives significant financing from large foundations, and it has several corporate executives on its board of directors (Dowie 1995, 58–59, 2001, 93; Roelofs 2003, 138–39). Susan R. Schrepfer, in her survey of the Sierra Club's early charter members, found that approximately one-third were academics, and "the rest of them were almost all businessmen and lawyers working in San Francisco's financial district" (1983, 10; also see Jones 1965; and Orsi 1985). The club was founded in 1892. Schrepfer goes on to explain that businesspeople continued to compose a substantial portion of the club's membership and leadership until the 1960s (1983, 171–73; also see Cohen 1988).

Unlike the Sierra Club, the high level of economic elite participation on Save-the-Redwoods League's governing council has been maintained throughout its history. The closed governance structure of the league created the "tendency for the council and board to be increasingly dominated by businessmen and patricians, while fewer academics were drawn into the organization's leadership in the 1950s and 1960s" (Schrepfer 1983, 113).

Environmental Defense, in particular, is a leader in what Mark Dowie (1995, ch. 5) calls third wave environmentalism. He views the advocates and adherents of this movement as conservative environmentalists because key in their thinking

> is the notion that production decisions should remain in the private sector and that removing market barriers and government subsidies that promote environmentally unsound practices will allow the mechanisms of the marketplace to motivate industries to make environmental protection profitable. (1995, 108)

Dowie goes on to argue that "another implicit tenet of the third-wave ideology is that all non-fraudulent businesses and industries deserve to exist, even if their technologies or products are irreversibly degrading to the environment" (1995, 108). Through their financing and participation in such organizations businesspeople can gain knowledge and policy proposals on environmental issues. Economic elites can then use this information and these policy proposals in their efforts to shape public policies on environmental questions when deemed necessary (Gonzalez 2001a, 2001b, 2005a, 2005b).

Economic elite–led policy discussion groups have also been formed for the purpose of shaping decision making on the urban level. One prominent example of such an entity is the National Municipal League (Hays 1964; Domhoff 1978b, 160–69). From the nationwide effort of this organization came the Progressive Era urban reforms of the civil service "to regulate personnel practices, competitive bidding to control procurement, the city manager form of government to systematize decision making, and at-large elections to dilute the voting power of the working classes" (Logan and Molotch 1987, 152).

## STATE IMPERATIVES, ECONOMIC ELITES, AND THE CAPITALIST ECONOMY

Returning to the issue of the imperatives of the state as elaborated by Dryzek, the economic elite approach would suggest that the state's imperatives are not determined within the state in response to different shifts in the operation of the political economy and/or public opinion. This view is implicit in the neo-Marxist view of politics (Barrow 1993, ch. 2; Dryzek 1996b; Aronowitz and Bratsis 2002; Wetherly 2005), as well as in state autonomy theory. Instead, it is economic elites and producer groups, operating through policy-planning networks, that determine which issues within capitalism are to be addressed by the state and how.

Various works on U.S. environmental policies support this position. It was economic elites, for example, both within the lumber industry and outside of it, that developed a forest management approach during turn of the twentieth century that prioritized profitability, as well as forest maintenance, in order to cope with a long-running glut of the timber market. The development and dissemination of this approach, known as "practical forestry," was heavily subsidized by the federal government (Gonzalez 1998, 2001a, ch. 2). Moreover, William G. Robbins (1982) and Paul Hirt (1994) demonstrate that the management of the national forests has historically been dictated by the lumber industry. This industry makes its demands upon government in response to fluctuations in the timber market. In the case of the national parks, economic elites led in the creation of the National Park Service so that tourism to the parks could be maximized. The national parks, in turn, became a more profitable outlet for capital investment for those economic sectors that economically benefit from this tourism (Runte 1997; Sellars 1997; Gonzalez 2001a, ch. 3; Barringer 2002; Louter 2006). Moreover, it was livestock firms, seeking land tenure stability, that led in the formulation of the federal government's policies managing grazing on the public grasslands (Foss 1960; Gonzalez 2001b).

# REGULATORY POLICIES, ECONOMIC ACTIVITY, AND ECONOMIC ELITES

Gabriel Kolko (1977), in his work on Progressive Era politics, demonstrates that economic elites and large firms can and do benefit from government regulatory policies. Such policies can protect the value of investments, stabilize the operation of the market, and enhance the long-term profitability of capital. In the realm of urban politics, Marc Weiss (1987) shows how local zoning laws, and regulations regarding the building of housing and retail structures, were championed by large land developers beginning in the Progressive Era. They did so to protect land values and local investment climates.

Despite these seminal works, and others like them (e.g., Stigler 1971; Gordon 1994; and Higgins-Evenson 2003), Barrow (1998) points out that it is assumed by numerous scholars who study state behavior that a negative relationship exists within jurisdictions between business investment and regulatory rules applied to business activities (e.g., Poulantzas 1973; Offe 1984; Block 1987; Elkin 1987; Aronowitz and Bratsis 2002; Hay, Lister, and Marsh 2006, ch. 3). Theorists that forward this view will normally link it to the "dependency principle," wherein it is posited that governments are reliant on private investment for a healthy economy and stable tax base (Offe 1974). Barrow explains that "in the literature on state theory, the operation of the dependency principle is always linked to a laissez-faire concept of the business climate and therefore to the basic presuppositions of neoclassical economic theory and the model of perfect competition" (111). Barrow goes on to point out that theorists of the state that argue the dependency principle generally equate a "favorable business climate" with:

> "low" taxes (and therefore minimal state expenditures); low employee mandates such as minimum wages, unemployment insurance, workmen's compensation, and family leave; minimal social regulation and environmental protection; right-to-work legislation to protect a "free" labor market and correspondingly low wages. (111)

Hence, public officials, in order to attract investment to their specific nation, region, or locality, must provide investors the type of low tax and low regulation milieu called for in neoclassical economic theory (Bartik 1991; Fisher and Peters 1998).

The linkage of the dependency principle to neoclassical thought, however, is empirically unwarranted. Neoclassical assumptions about business investment prove to be poor predictors of where investment and economic growth in the United States occur. The General Manufacturing Climates, for example, was a ten-year effort (1979–1988) to "operationalize neoclassical assumptions through an index that compares and ranks business climates in the 48 contiguous American states" (Barrow 1998, 112). It was sponsored by the Conference of State Manufacturers' Associations (COSMA). The General Manufacturing Climates used the "Grant Thornton index" to measure a favorable business climate based on "low wages, low union density, high work force availability (i.e., high unemployment), conservative state and local fiscal policies, and low state-mandated employment costs" (Barrow 1998, 112). In explaining the failure of this index to predict the national patterns of economic investment and growth, Barrow points out that its rankings

> were always inconsistent with perceived realities since North Dakota, Nebraska, and South Dakota ranked among the top three business climates year after year. Likewise, during the 1980s, California (30), Connecticut (35), and Rhode Island (37)

ranked well below the median even though these states were in the midst of a robust expansion of business activity, employment, and personal income growth. (112)

Other studies testing the reliability of the Grant Thornton index found it significantly lacking in its ability to explain patterns of economic activity and investment in the United States (Lane, Clennon, and McCabe 1989; Kozlowski and Weekly 1990).

Barrow proffers a different way to conceptualize business climates and the role of governments in creating a "positive" investment climate. He specifically rejects the neoclassical approach, which conceptualizes economic activity as a series of "abstract market exchanges" that occur without effort, without friction, and without a legal framework. Instead, Barrow argues cogently that

in terms of constructing a concept of business climate, the taxes and fees that support public infrastructure, public education, and state-regulated employee mandates should all be regarded as transaction costs. They are part of the cost of creating and using markets. (117) (also see Ely 1914; Commons 1924; Coase 1960; Higgins-Evenson 2003)

Therefore, as opposed to viewing public infrastructures and various regulations as a drain on private firms and economic activity, such infrastructures and regulations should be viewed as a complex matrix that facilitates the operation of the market and economic activity.

With this view of the relationship between regulatory frameworks and economic activity, the economic elite approach would indicate that economic elites strive to implement those regulatory frameworks that protect and enhance economic activity and their market position. Historically, it has been demonstrated that economic elites will promote environmental regulations when they view it in their economic and/or political interest to do so. Casner (1999), for example, demonstrates that the Pennsylvania Railroad in the 1920s successfully advocated the regulation of water pollution from coal mines in Pennsylvania in order to protect its train lines from said pollution. Next I outline how economic elites in the United States have historically sought to develop growth-enhancing regulations to abate localized air pollution.

## ECONOMIC ELITES AND CLEAN AIR

Economic elites will utilize policy-planning organizations to formulate the "appropriate" regulations, and to achieve political consensus on such issues. During the late nineteenth and early twentieth centuries, for example, the Chicago Association of Commerce (CAC) and the Society for the Prevention of Smoke (SPS) took up the issue of the large amounts of smoke that were inundating the city of Chicago during this period, and ostensibly hurting its business climate. Both organizations were composed of prominent Chicago businesspeople (Walker 1941; Rosen 1986). The CAC sought to address the smoke that was emanating from the railroads that ran throughout the city. These railroads were heavy users of highly polluting bituminous (or soft) coal. The SPS undertook an effort to abate smoke from stationary sources in anticipation of the upcoming Chicago World's Fair of 1893. Like the railroads, factories burned large amounts of bituminous (i.e., "dirty") coal (Gonzalez 2005a, ch. 3).

In private meetings between railroad executives and CAC members, the executives made it clear that they were opposed to efforts to electrify their railroad lines for purposes of air pollution abatement (Stradling and Tarr 1999). With the railroads serving as the key factor underlying Chicago's economic growth during this period (Hoyt 1933; Pred 1966, 54), the CAC backed off its effort to have the city's railroads electrified. In the case of SPS's smoke abatement efforts, the technology available to abate smoke from the burning of coal was unreliable and labor intensive (Stradling 1999), and shortly after the start of the Chicago World's Fair the SPS ended its campaign for smoke abatement (Rosen 1986).

In the mid-1950s when Los Angeles' air quality severely deteriorated (Brienes 1975, 1976), members from the business community formed the Air Pollution Foundation, and examined the role of the automobile in the creation of Los Angeles' smog. The automobile by the 1920s had become the key means through which land developers in Los Angeles would bring utility to their landholdings outside of the city center, thereby making such land useful as sites for housing, industrial production, and retail space (Weiss 1987; Hise 1997; Gonzalez 2005a, ch. 4). As a result, Los Angeles had the highest per capita automobile ownership in the country (Foster 1975). The foundation's board of trustees was composed of representatives from local economic interests and from firms of the national automotive industry (e.g., the Big Three automakers, oil companies, and tire manufacturers). It also enjoyed broad funding from the U.S. corporate community (Air Pollution Foundation 1961, 50–56).

The foundation in 1956 politically established that the automobile was the principal cause of Los Angeles' smog situation (Krier and Ursin 1977, 86; Dewey 2000, ch. 4). In terms of the control of automobile exhaust, the foundation's answer was technology. It centered its air pollution abatement "research program" on the "development of scientific principles upon which effective exhaust control devices could be used" (Air Pollution Foundation 1961, 29).

Local growth coalitions are composed of economic interests that financially benefit from local growth (Logan and Molotch 1987). A technological approach to abating localized air pollution is directly in line with the financial interests of local growth coalitions. This is because the deployment of technology to improve air quality does not directly interfere with these coalitions' efforts to attract more investment and economic activity to their areas, nor does it interfere with landholders' and developers' efforts to use the automobile to bring utility to their holdings. Therefore, the successful implementing of technology to abate air pollution can serve to enhance local economic growth and real estate values, in that improved air quality improves a local investment clime. (It is important to note that locally oriented economic elites do not have the same incentives to abate carbon dioxide emissions as they do smoke from the burning of coal or smog from the widespread use of automobile. Unlike smoke or smog, carbon dioxide is odorless and invisible.)

In the contemporary period, leading members of California's business community have formed the California Council for Environmental and Economic Balance (CCEEB) to shape the state's environmental regulations. This organization was established in 1973. One-third of its board of directors is drawn from business and industry. Some of the firms represented on CCEEB's board are economically dependent on growth in the state. They are the Irvine Company (real estate and land development), Pacific Telesis (regional telephone service provider), Southern California Edison (utility firm), Bank of America, and Pacific Gas & Electric Company. Other firms represented on CCEEB's board are directly affected by the state's environmental regulations. These firms include ChevronTexaco and the Union Pacific Railroad. The other two-thirds of the board is composed of labor union representatives and private citizens.[5] The CCEEB's finances are entirely provided by its corporate members (Weisser 2000). Moreover, CCEEB disseminates its policy ideas throughout the California business community through "presentations" to such organizations as the Los Angeles Chamber of Commerce, the Santa Clara Manufacturers Group, and the Orange County Industrial League (CCEEB 2000). Like the Air Pollution Foundation before it, the CCEEB advocates the use of technological controls to improve local air quality (Gonzalez 2005a, ch. 6).

It is because members of local growth coalitions have historically sought to shape clean air regulations in a way that enhances local growth that studies find a positive statistical correlation between "strong" air pollution rules and economic activity on the state level. In other words, what studies have found is that states with high levels of economic activity also tend to be the states with the strongest clean air rules. California, for instance, is the wealthiest state in the United States, and it also implements the strictest set of clean air rules (Game 1979; Lowry 1992; Ringquist 1993; Potoski 2001).

It is also important to note that a reliance on technology to abate pollution is politically reassuring to industrial firms. This is because it is these firms that control the development and deployment of such technology. Thus, any policies that rely on pollution abatement technologies rely on industrial firms to develop and deploy these technologies. In this way, industrial firms are central in making and implementation those policies that utilize pollution abatement technologies (Noble 1977; Davison 2001; Hornborg 2001). For such firms, a reliance on technology to abate pollution is a much more politically palatable approach than one, for example, that would seek to dictate production schedules, or one that seeks to curb demand for products that create environmentally deleterious airborne emissions when used (e.g., automobiles).

## CONCLUSION

Plural elite theory can be deployed to explain the development of urban sprawl in the United States. As I will describe in the next chapter, urban sprawl techniques were pioneered by the real estate industry in the 1920s, especially in California. During the Great Depression in the 1930s, the federal government launched a housing program to help revive the economy, and prominent officials from this industry and the financial sector were placed in charge of this program. As a result, the government agency entrusted with implementing the government's housing program, the FHA, promoted and subsidized sprawled urban development throughout the postwar period.

The pro–urban sprawl policies of the United States have persisted in the face of the environmental social movement, the oil crises of the 1970s, and global warming. This indicates that there is a deep commitment to urban sprawl—beyond the maneuvering of specific special interests. It would appear that beginning with the 1930s urban sprawl became an imperative of the state, and the real estate and financial sectors have been used to implement this imperative.

The salient question then becomes, Who has set this imperative? The state autonomy approach offers one means through which to analyze state behavior in response to the various political controversies created by the operation of capitalism—including that of climate change. According to this view of policy formulation, officials within the state take the political lead in addressing such controversies and determining state objectives. Economic elite theory offers a substantially different view of the policymaking process than that of state autonomy theory. Here, economic elites, and not public officials, are at the center of the policymaking process. Operating through policy-planning networks, economic elites determine what types and which policies will forward their economic and political interests. They, in turn, utilize their superior political means to ensure that the resources and organizational techniques that comprise the state are deployed to correspond to their preferred policies. In doing so, economic elites forward those public policies that they believe serve their interests and block those they perceive do not.

In the chapters that follow I will describe how urban sprawl became a key means to increase the consumption of consumer durables in the United States. Within this context of urban sprawl serving as a mainstay of the global economy, oil became and remains a vital resource. The rise of urban sprawl in the United States, and the elevation of oil to a key strategic resource, is consistent with the economic elite approach to public policy formation. As the link between urban sprawl and climate change has become more apparent, international business groups have sought to address climate change through the development and deployment of technology. In this way, such groups hope that the urban sprawl approach to economic prosperity can be maintained and the climate change trend mitigated or eliminated. As I have outlined in this chapter, this reliance on technology to deal with airborne emissions is consistent with how the U.S. business community has historically sought to deal with such emissions.

# Chapter Three

# Real Estate Interests and the Techniques of Urban Sprawl

Prominent arguments used to explain why U.S. cities are so sprawled (as outlined in chapter 1) are rooted in culture and consumer preferences. The claim, for instance, is made that U.S. residents desire to live in relatively spacious single-family homes and in low-density neighborhoods (Baxandall and Ewen 2000; Conte 2000; Gillham 2002; Avila 2004; Bruegmann 2005; Bogart 2006). Cotton Seiler (2003) in a critical analysis of U.S. political culture during the cold war holds that a particular notion of freedom and liberty was promoted in the United States by political, economic, and cultural elites. He specifically argues that in the post–World War II period a concept of freedom was emphasized that centered on the automobile and the seemingly absolute freedom of movement that it offered (also see Rajan 1996). Seiler holds that this concept was posited as a way to differentiate the United States from the Soviet Union. Urban sprawl became consistent with automobile-centered freedom, insofar as the notion of freedom associated with the automobile was tied to the ability to partake of goods and services virtually everywhere people went in their cars.

While Americans may desire to live in spacious homes and in low-density neighborhoods, it does not explain why U.S. cities are by far the most sprawled in the world. In contrast to their U.S. counterparts, do Europeans generally desire to live in smaller abodes and in higher density urban zones? If so, it is not clear why. Additionally, as I noted in chapter 1 and outlined below, urban sprawl in the United States was initiated not during the post–World War II period nor with the advent of the automobile, but in the late nineteenth century with the development of the streetcar (i.e., the electric trolley) (Dewees 1970; Cheape 1980; Foster 1981; Gonzalez 2005a, ch. 4). Furthermore, also described below, automobile-centered urban sprawl was evident in the United States during the 1920s. Also described in the next chapter is the fact that the key political/policy decisions that would serve as the basis for the sprawling of urban development throughout the country were made in 1930s.

These key decisions were predicated on two factors: (1) the salient features of the U.S. economy during the early twentieth century, and (2) the United States' historic access to oil supplies. The first factor is treated at length in the next chapter, and the second is taken up in chapter 5. The salient features of the U.S. economy that facilitated/prompted urban sprawl in the United States were an abundance of capital and an industrial base geared toward the production of consumer durables, especially automobiles.

While economic elites from the industrial and financial communities reaped substantial and important benefits from the sprawling of urban America, the techniques of urban sprawl were developed by local growth coalitions (especially land developers) during the late nineteenth and early twentieth century (the subject of this chapter). Land developers were entrusted with governing the Federal Housing Authority (described in the next chapter). In the post–World War II era this agency implemented key pro–urban sprawl policies. Economic elites were also directly involved in the creation of the Federal Housing Authority and its policies (discussed in the next chapter).

Therefore, the analysis here is consistent with the economic elite approach to public policy development and state behavior. As outlined in chapter 2, those who hold this view contend that economic elites and producer groups are at the center of public policy formation. Moreover, the argument offered here supports the view that historical analysis can have significant explanatory power with regard to contemporary and ongoing political phenomena (Pierson 2000; Büthe 2002).

This chapter begins with a description of the role of local growth coalitions in U.S. land politics—with an emphasis on Chicago and Los Angeles. I then outline how these growth coalitions used modern means of transportation—starting with the trolley and including the automobile—to bring utility to land on the urban periphery, and in the process horizontally pushed out urban growth. By the 1920s horizontal urban development was most evident in Los Angeles.

# LOCAL GROWTH COALITIONS AND U.S. LAND POLITICS

As explained in chapter 2, local growth coalitions are composed of economic interests that financially benefit from local economic growth (Mollenkopf 1983; Logan and Molotch 1987; Jonas and Wilson 1999; Drier, Mollenkopf, and Swanstrom 2001). The central members of these coalitions are large landholders and land developers. Economic growth in a specific region serves to increase the value of land in said region, because expanding economic activity in an area normally translates into higher demand, and hence higher prices, for land. Also, members of local growth coalitions are businesses that specifically benefit from the local expansion of the consumer base. These businesses include local media outlets and utilities (Molotch 1976, 1979; Bowles, Gordon, Weisskopf 1983).

Local growth coalitions and their considerable influence over urban growth and development in the United States are in part the result of the liberal land and economic development policies pursued by the U.S. government from its inception, which continued the liberal land policies of the British imperial regime. Under this regime, land was freely distributed to land speculators and settlers. In contrast, Spain, for example, tended to grant large tracts of land to individuals favored by the crown. Moreover, much of Spain's economic development was directed from Madrid in order to directly increase the imperial government's revenue (Allen 2000; Weaver 2003; Elliott 2006; Mackin 2006).

With generally open land policies, a multitude of individuals, along with the railroads, during the nineteenth century headed out into the U.S. frontier to exploit and profit from its natural resources. As a result of this activity, cities arose to facilitate the extraction of these resources and their shipment to central cities in the northeastern United States and Western and Central Europe. Frontier cities also served as the means to distribute finished goods to the hinterland. Over time, many of these cities also became major centers of production and consumption themselves (Pred 1966, 1980; Cronon 1991; Robbins 1994; Moehring 2004; Abbott 2008).

Local growth coalitions have contributed significantly to the evolution of the U.S. city system, and, consequently, to the effective operation of capitalism in the United States. This is in contrast to the position of David Ricardo (1830) and thinkers of his ilk (Foley 2003), who view profits derived from landownership as a rent, or unearned gain, expropriated through control of a strategic asset. Instead, as David Harvey (1985) avers, large landowners and developers, along with their allies who economically benefit from local growth, play an important role in the capital accumulation process. This is because local growth coalitions lead in the provision of the physical, legal, and political factors required for the profitable production and distribution of commodities (Jaher 1982; Eisinger 1988; Stone 1989). As a result, cities become venues where aggregations of labor and capital are brought together in a profitable manner (Harvey 1985; Barrow 1998), as well as places where raw materials, goods, and services can be profitably transported and exchanged (Moehring 2004).

The rise of Chicago as a major transit point and manufacturing area of the United States demonstrates how local growth coalitions play key roles in shaping regions into areas that are conducive to economic activity, and, ultimately, capital accumulation. In addition to geographic factors, Chicago became a good place for capital investment, including that from railroads, during the middle and late nineteenth century because local actors created the physical and political milieu conducive for such investment.

With the clearing out of the Native American population, and the institution of cheap credit, Chicago during the 1830s became part of the broader effort to profit from the expected colonization of the Old Northwest territory. Historian William Cronon (1991) explains that

> the mid-1830s saw the most intense land speculation in American history, with Chicago at the center of the vortex. Believing Chicago was about to become the terminus of a major canal, land agents and speculators flooded into town, buying and selling not only the empty lots along its ill-marked streets but also the surrounding grasslands which the Indians had recently abandoned. (29)

Therefore, once the Indian population was moved out, thereby opening the Old Northwest territory to be integrated into the U.S. and European economies, inhabitants and investors in significant numbers came to the Chicago area to economically benefit from an anticipated land boom. Frederic Jaher (1982) has written an extensive history of the leading political and economic circles in several U.S. cities. In describing the upper socioeconomic stratum of Chicago during the nineteenth century, he referred to it as a "multifunctional elite," whose "members formed the first banks and insurance, manufacturing, and utility companies, and pioneered in retail and wholesale trade, transportation ventures, and real estate operations" (456). The pro-growth views of this class of Chicago residents and investors came to dominate the city's politics (Belcher 1947; Keating 1988).

The predominance of a pro-growth political outlook led to various projects designed to attract capital investment to the area. For example, it facilitated the building of a canal in the 1840s that connected Lake Michigan to the Mississippi River watershed, thereby making the Chicago area an important North American transport point (Belcher 1947, 34–35; Cronon 1991, 32–33). Moreover, in the late 1840s, it was leading members of Chicago's real estate interests that built the first railroad line running to Chicago (Belcher 1947, 125–31; Cronon 1991, 65–67). In the 1850s, Illinois Senator Stephen Douglas, who himself held substantial tracts of land in the area (Belcher 1947, 125–26), successfully lobbied to have the first federal railroad land grant run to Chicago (Cronon 1991, 68–70).

This congenial attitude toward investment and economic growth in Chicago paid off well for those that owned substantial amounts of land in the area. Jaher (1982) notes that when the town was platted in 1830, the heaviest taxpayers of the previous decade or their relatives purchased the lion's share of Chicago's first land sale. The successful arrivals of the 1830s and '40s also began as real estate speculators. [William B.] Odgen, the town's foremost real estate dealer, [Gurdon S.] Hubbard, [John] Wentworth, Walter L. Newberry, and others founded their fortunes on profitable land transactions. (457)

Between the years 1833 and 1910, land value within the incorporated area of Chicago had grown from $168,000 to $1.5 billion. By 1926, the eve of the Great Depression, total land value in Chicago equaled $5 billion (Hoyt 1933, 470; also see Keating 1988).

Los Angeles serves perhaps as an even better example of a local growth coalition providing the factors necessary for technological innovation and productive activity (Erie 2004, 2006). This is most evident in the establishment of Los Angeles as a center of airplane manufacturing during the middle part of the twentieth century (Lotchin 1992; Hise 1997, 2001). In his book *Fortress California: 1910–1960*, Roger Lotchin (1992) describes how the financial, physical, and labor variables necessary to entice aircraft investment to the region, and to ensure its success, were provided, in large part, by Los Angeles business leaders. Lotchin, in the following, summarizes some of his findings:

> If the plane makers desperately lacked capital, Security Pacific, Brashears, or some private Southland investor provided it when San Francisco or New York City would not. If the industry profited from its proximity to several of the foremost centers of military aviation technology, the boosters [of Los Angeles] had earlier secured these assets. If [plane manufacturers] Douglas, Lockheed, North American, Consolidated, Vultee, and Ryan wanted a cheap and docile labor force, their booster friends did their best to develop and prolong its presence. . . . If the increasingly technological character of the aeronautical industry demanded easy and ever-growing access to both the material and intellectual resources of the scientific community . . . [the California Institute of Technology in Los Angeles] would eventually provide its own airplane testing facilities and then be called upon to manage both the Southern California Cooperative Wind Tunnel and the Jet Propulsion Laboratory. (130)

Lotchin adds that "if an industry largely dependent upon the government for a market [in the form of military contracts] cried out for political influence (and who can doubt that it did?), [southern California] urban politicians from the stature of United States senators down to the city planning commissions stood ready to mobilize it" (130; parentheses in original).

Particularly germane for this discussion, given that one of its foci is airborne emissions in the form of greenhouse gases, is the role of local growth coalition members in the abatement of localized air pollution. As I described in chapter 2, local growth coalitions have historically taken the lead in efforts to reduce air pollution. They have done so because acute air pollution negatively affects a city's business climate. As a result, local economic interests have historically placed political pressure on business and industry to ecologically modernize through the deployment of technology (Gonzalez 2005a). Technological controls on air pollution are consistent with local growth coalitions' economic and political interests because such controls help to abate localized air pollution without directly interfering with the goal of maximizing local economic growth. Hence, local growth coalitions have historically taken the political lead in seeking to provide salutary air so that production and consumption processes can briskly proceed.

It is important to stress that local growth coalitions do not have the same incentives to abate the emissions of greenhouse gases, especially carbon dioxide, as they do other forms of airborne emission. Present in large enough quantities, smog (largely from automobile emissions) and smoke (or sulfur dioxide from the burning of coal) create obvious aesthetic blights and health risks, and areas inundated with such pollution become less desirable places to live, work, and invest. Carbon dioxide, in contrast to smoke and smog, is invisible and odorless.

Apart from their efforts to convert their specific area and region into a growth machine, local growth coalitions in the United States have historically been a driving force behind the sprawling of urban development. This is because horizontal development pushes up the value of land at the urban periphery. As such, large land developers fostered the techniques and public policies necessary to move urban development away from the city center. In their efforts to do so, the automobile became an important tool, and they shaped urban and suburban development around this tool. Even prior to the popularization of the automobile, however, American real estate interests were sprawling urban development. They were doing so through the trolley.

## THE EARLY HISTORY OF URBAN SPRAWL IN THE UNITED STATES

Urban sprawl in the United States was initially spurred by the advent of the electrified streetcar, or trolley, in the late nineteenth century. In many important instances the trolley in the United States was utilized more as a means to derive wealth from landholdings on the urban periphery than as a means to provide efficient and cost-effective transportation in urban centers.

This is most clearly the case in the Los Angeles metropolitan area. It was Henry E. Huntington who financed the trolley system that was eventually deployed throughout the Los Angeles region during the first decade of the twentieth century (Bottles 1987; Crump 1988). Huntington had inherited a fortune from his uncle, Colis Huntington—a cofounder of the Southern Pacific railroad—estimated at $50 million (Crump 1988, 42). He invested much of this fortune in real estate throughout the region and in the trolley system—the Pacific Electric and Los Angeles Railway. The system was primarily developed as a way to inflate the value of Huntington's real estate holdings.

Huntington undertook his real estate purchasing efforts in the Los Angeles region during a time when it was a still a fledgling metropolitan area and had a relatively small population. Hence, he obtained large tracts of land relatively inexpensively, but these tracts were also widely dispersed throughout the region. Spencer Crump (1988), historian of Huntington's interurban trolley system, the Pacific Electric, in the following describes how Huntington would select where to run his trolley lines and acquire his landholdings:

> Huntington's instinctive business foresight, not a battery of professional economists frequently used by financial tycoons, was his instrument in choosing the areas where his trolleys—and his investments in substantial land holdings—would go. Climbing a knoll, he would inspect the countryside and visualize the logical course for an area's pattern of development. (60)

Utilizing this method, Huntington obtained scattered landholdings throughout southern California. He also deployed a far-flung trolley system, which one historian of urban mass transit referred to as "the most extensive interurban [trolley] system in the world" (Foster 1981, 17). This system would disperse economic activity and residential housing throughout the region, and would presage the highly diffuse urban development that has characterized the Los Angeles region throughout the twentieth century and into the contemporary era (Fogelson 1967; Viehe 1981; Hise 1997; Fulton 2001). Crump (1988) argues that when the Los Angeles trolley cars "finally rolled into the realm of history [in 1961], they left a sprawling City of Southern California built precisely as it was because the rail lines had encouraged just that development" (115–16).

The utilization of rapid transit to enhance land values and create urban sprawl was not unique to Los Angeles. The positive relationship between land values and rapid transportation had long been understood (Jackson 1985; Stilgoe 1988). During most of the nineteenth century, however, walking remained the primary means of getting around in urban settings, and as a result cities were relatively compact and often highly congested (Rosen 1986; Schultz 1989).

Early rapid transportation methods were of limited utility. Carriages and omnibuses were reliant on horse power, which severely limited their range and speed. Moreover, the costs of such modes of transportation restricted their use to affluent city dwellers. The first methods of mechanized urban transportation had limited utility for economic and/or political reasons. The use of steam engines within urban areas was resisted in part because residents feared that they would explode. Additionally, the noise and air pollution emitted by such engines tended to depress the value of adjacent property. Also, their long stopping distance, or headway, undermined their usefulness for urban transport. The other early approach to the mechanization of urban transportation was the cable car. Its high initial and maintenance costs, however, confined its use to only the most densely populated areas (McShane 1994).

The trolley did not have the same liabilities as horses, steam engines, or cable cars. Trolleys could move at fairly rapid speeds. Given initial costs and maintenance expenses, trolley systems were relatively inexpensive to run. Trolley cars were also clean and largely noiseless. Thus, soon after their successful demonstration in Richmond, Virginia, in 1887, trolley cars were used in numerous urban areas throughout the United States, including New York, Boston, Philadelphia, Chicago, and Milwaukee (McShane 1974, 1994; Warner 1978; Cheape 1980; Foster 1981; Barrett 1983; Fogelson 2001, ch. 2).

Trolley lines throughout the United States, like those in Los Angeles, were used to increase the value of outlying land. Indeed, the first trolley system in a major metropolitan area was actually developed as part of a massive land development plan (Cheape 1980, 115). Led by Henry M. Whitney, the investors of the West End Land Company sought to develop five million square feet of land on Boston's outskirts. The trolley was the only means to make this subdivided land available to the buyers the company hoped to attract. In order to connect its landholdings with the rest of the city, the investors of the West End Land Company were forced through their subsidiary, the West End Street Railway, to take over the franchises of other transit lines, and subsequently integrated them into a citywide trolley system in the mid-1890s. Historian Charles Cheape (1980) notes with some irony that in Boston, "what had begun as an adjunct to a real estate venture became a major transit enterprise" (115). More generally, Mark S. Foster (1981), a historian of rapid transit in the United States, notes that "in the late nineteenth century, real estate interests and trolley promoters combined to develop huge areas of Brooklyn, Boston, Chicago, and many other large cities" (17).

In the next section, I shift our attention specifically to the rise of automobile-centered urban sprawl in the United States. As the automobile became ever more popularized (Flink 1975, 1990), land developers by the 1920s increasingly planned with cars in mind in order to bring utility to land on the urban periphery. In doing so, they substantially increased low-density urban development in the United States. This was especially the case in the city of Los Angeles.

## THE AUTOMOBILE AND THE TECHNIQUES OF URBAN SPRAWL

Marc Weiss (1987), in his instructive work on modern low-density urban planning techniques, explains that such techniques were developed by large land developers in order to protect and enhance their large-scale housing developments. Weiss points out that "subdividers who engaged in full-scale community development . . . performed the function of being private planners for American cities and towns." He goes on to write that

> working together with professional engineers, landscape architects, building architects, and other urban designers, residential real estate developers worked out "on the ground" many of the concepts and forms that came to be accepted as good planning. The classification and design of major and minor streets, the superblock and cul-de-sac, planting strips and rolling topography, arrangement of the house on the lot, lot size and shape, set-back lines and lot coverage restrictions, planned separation and relation of multiple uses, design and placement of parks and recreational amenities, ornamentation, easements, underground utilities, and numerous other physical features were first introduced by private developers and later adopted as rules and principles by public planning agencies. (3; also see Hornstein 2005)

Many of the largest and most innovative land developers "did more than just serve as innovators for the land planning ideas that were spawned in the early 1900s, and spread rapidly during the succeeding four decades." Instead, "many of the large subdivision developers played a direct role in actively supporting and shaping the emerging system of public land planning and land-use regulation" (4). Consistent with economic elite theory (as described in chapter 2), they did so in conjunction with policy-planning groups. Leading examples of such groups include the Home Builders and Subdividers Division and the City Planning Committee of the National Association of Real Estate Boards (NAREB). As Weiss explains, most of those large developers, whom he refers to as "community builders," involved in shaping government regulations on land use during the early twentieth century "developed stylish and expensive residential subdivisions and were leaders" of this division and committee within NAREB. Significantly,

> beginning in 1914, a group of community builders from NAREB's City Planning Committee exchanged ideas with the landscape architects, civil engineers, architects and lawyers who predominated in the National Conference of City Planning (NCCP), founded in 1909. Together, these community builders and NCCP activists worked to promote planning legislation among other entrepreneurs, in the real estate industry, to the general public, and within the state and local governments. (Weiss 1987, 56)

Large land developers sought to shape public policies on land use issues because:

> Private developers who scrupulously planned and regulated their own subdivisions needed the planning and regulation of the surrounding private and public land in order to maintain cost efficiencies and transportation accessibility and to ensure a stable and high-quality, long-term environment for their prospective property owners. (4)

A central objective of large developers in championing urban planning during the early twentieth century was to accommodate the automobile. Weiss points out that one of the key factors in promoting large-scale community building and the subsequent drive for private and public urban planning was "the increasing availability of private automobiles for upper- and middle-income [home] purchasers" (62). Hence, the accommodation of the automobile in urban and suburban areas, as well as building homes that could accommodate automobiles, became central to reorganizing urban areas and organizing new suburbs.

Paul Barrett (1983), for instance, documents how in Chicago the business community generally supported the use of the automobile and the outward expansion it brought during the early part of the twentieth century (also see Smith 2006).[1] Additionally, Blaine A. Brownell (1975), who studied urban public opinion in the South between 1920 and 1930 by examining major newspapers in the region, points out that Southern "businessmen lauded the automobile because it promised to open up new channels of commerce, expand the pool of customers for downtown merchants, and make available large expanses of outlying territory for urban growth and economic development." He adds:

The major issue concerning businessmen in major southern cities during the 1920s was not whether the automobile was desirable, but whether roads, highways, and related facilities could be provided rapidly enough to insure the maximum degree of economic advantage. The Good Roads Movement in the South, and throughout the country, had always received the support of prominent business groups, and in the 1920s most chambers of commerce in the larger cities established committees especially charged with the task of promoting highway construction and the repair of existing roads. (117)

Howard Preston (1991), who wrote a history on the development of roads in the South during the late nineteenth and early twentieth centuries, adds that "by 1915 the legions of good roads apostles in the South were swollen with chamber of commerce members, bank presidents, sales representatives, real estate agents, and trade board members" (41).

Land developers in the Los Angeles region led the way in the urban planning field. The region's sparse population, the fact that developers could purchase large tracts of land relatively inexpensively, and the widely dispersed trolley system (Bottles 1987; Crump 1988) meant that Los Angeles was an ideal area to launch large-scale community developments by individual developers. As a result, many of the urban planning techniques and public policies discussed in this chapter were initially developed and applied in Los Angeles (Weiss 1987; Hise 1997).

Los Angeles developers, at the cutting edge of community development methods, were quick to see the profit potential in the automobile, and planned and developed accordingly. As a result, the mass production of the automobile, and the urban planning methods developed and politically sponsored by large developers to accommodate the automobile, profoundly affected Los Angeles. Historian Mark S. Foster (1975) points out that

> while the trolley promoters established a number of subdivisions miles from the downtown area, they had developed only a tiny fraction of the land in the Los Angeles area by 1920. Pre–World War I residents were so dependent upon the trolley for transportation that developers made few attempts to promote single-family homesites more than a half-mile from the lines. (476)

The declining cost of the automobile (à la Ford and later General Motors [Farber 2002] and Chrysler [Curcio 2000]; see chapter 4 of this book), and the growing public confidence in it (Flink 1975, 1990), however, "exerted a dramatic effect on the remote areas which were not so well served by the trolleys." Foster explains that

[t]he development of the San Fernando Valley during the 1920s was, perhaps, the most spectacular example. The real estate boom of the 1920s witnessed the promotion of thousands of lots, many located miles from the nearest trolley lines. The Encino tract, opened in 1923, contained several hundred single-family home-sites. The development was located on the southwest corner of Balboa and Ventura boulevards, two miles from the nearest red [trolley] car stop. The Girard tract—which contained several thousand single-family homesites—was situated even further from the trolley lines, the nearest line being almost three miles distant. These were but two of the many subdivisions opened during the 1920s in the valley where residents generally relied upon the automobile for their transportation. (477)

As a result, by the end of the 1920s the Los Angeles area had become the U.S. region most adapted to the automobile, whereby "residents of Los Angeles purchased more automobiles per capita than did residents of any other city in the country." During this period "there were two automobiles for every five residents in Los Angeles, compared to one for every four residents in Detroit, the next most 'automobile oriented' American city" (Foster 1975, 483).

## CONCLUSION

Landed interests in the United States have historically undertaken projects that have had the benefit of increasing local economic growth and local property values. Chicago's establishment as the second city of the United States during the late nineteenth century can be directly attributable to the activity of its landed and local business elites. In the city of Los Angeles the region's economic interests sought to push up land values through industrialization and the sprawling of land development. This sprawling initially occurred through the use of the trolley and then by the 1920s through automobile-centered urban planning. Therefore, as described in the next chapter, when federal policymakers decided to promote automobile-centered urban sprawl to resuscitate the economy in the 1930s, U.S. land developers had already fostered the urban planning techniques that made this possible.

Neither large landholders, land developers, the techniques of sprawl, nor the automobile are unique to the United States. Thus, while they may be necessary conditions for the sprawling of urban development, these factors to do not explain why U.S. urban areas became substantially more sprawled than other cities throughout the world. For that explanation, we must look to the salient features of the U.S. economy prior to World War II. Two key aspects of the U.S. economy during the interwar period served to prod urban development in a horizontal direction: (1) the surplus capital the United States had accumulated, and (2) the fact that U.S. industrial capacity was predominantly geared toward the production of durable consumer goods—especially the automobile. Federal housing policy, beginning in the 1930s, brought these factors together to create the highly sprawled urban zones of the United States.

# Chapter Four

# The Federal Government and the National Establishment of Urban Sprawl

In the last chapter I outlined how the techniques of urban sprawl were developed by land developers seeking to bring utility to their landholdings outside of the city center. By the 1920s these techniques centered on the automobile. Among major U.S. cities, it was Los Angeles that was most profoundly shaped by the automobile-centered techniques of urban sprawl during this period. Elsewhere in the United States, urban transportation was dominated by the trolley and walking, which served to limit the market for the economically important automobile.

During the Great Depression, however, two factors combined to radically reshape urban zones throughout the United States and render them automobile dependent: an abundance of capital and federal policies promoting suburban development. In this chapter I explain how and why these factors combined to produce the United States' highly sprawled cities. This explanation is laid out in four sections:

1. The first section of this chapter outlines how leading members of the U.S. financial sector in the context of the Depression sought to make the domestic real estate market a more reliable and profitable outlet for surplus capital.

2. The second section describes how consumer durables production was the salient feature of the U.S. industrial base by the 1920s, and how this consumer durables–oriented manufacturing infrastructure was particularly geared toward producing automobiles. Consumer durables are goods intended to last three years or more.

3. The third section of this chapter explains how federal housing policy in the 1930s was shaped by economic elites to spur suburban sprawl in order to profitably absorb the United States' surplus capital and consumer durables industrial output.

4. The fourth and final section delineates how urban sprawl in the United States spawned a consumer durables revolution, whereby the consumption of these commodities exceeded wage growth and served as a basis for the post–World War II economic boom.

## SURPLUS CAPITAL

By the 1920s the U.S. economy held a substantial amount of surplus capital. In 1929 approximately $52 billion was held in bank savings and other deposits. As one observer notes, funds in banks, saving and loans, and other commercial lenders from 1900 to 1929 "grew about three times as fast as the overall economy" (Stone 1980, 80).

Much of this excess capital was utilized to underwrite the allied war effort during World War I through loans. In the post-armistice aftermath, the United States was the primary source of funds for the European economies seeking to recover from the war and pay war reparations. As a result of this lending activity, the United States became the world's largest creditor nation. With the onset of the Depression in 1929, however, the international flow of capital collapsed, as countries, including those in Western and Central Europe, found it difficult to impossible to cover outstanding debts (Fearon 1987, ch. 7). Moreover, with the crash of the stock market, brokerage loans declined substantially. Loans that were issued against stocks dropped from a high of $7 billion in June 1929 to $1.6 by June 1931, and later to $335 million by June 1932 (Fearon 1987, 119).

Within the context of the Depression, leading members of the U.S. banking and investment community sought to make domestic real estate into a more reliable outlet for capital. This was reflected in the President's Conference on Home Building and Home Ownership held in 1931. A Committee on Finance (which ostensibly became an economic elite policy-planning group) was convened as part of the conference. Among the committee's members were executives from the United States Building and Loan League (a trade organization), Dillon, Read, and Company (a key investment firm), Metropolitan Life Insurance, New York Title and Mortgage Company, Southern Trust Company, American Loan and Savings Association (a major home mortgage lender), and the American Bankers Association (a trade organization). Also on this committee was the president of the National Association of Real Estate Boards (NAREB) (Gries and Ford 1932, v).

The committee's report focused on the residential real estate market. Its authors noted that "instability in home property values was confirmed as a major difficulty by the committee's studies." Importantly, "financial institutions have a vital stake in the stability of real estate values in any territory where they operate" (Gries and Ford 1932, 22). The committee made two key recommendations in order to bring stability to the residential real estate market: an appropriate down payment and long-term amortized loans.

The committee advised "that a down payment of about 25 per cent of the purchase price should be established as the basis of a sound home purchase transaction" (Gries and Ford 1932, 23). The committee's authors noted that at the time "most of the savings institutions that lend on first mortgages operate on conservative principles, and it has been customary for them to limit their loans to from 40 to 60 per cent of appraised value" (Gries and Ford 1932, 25–26). A down payment of 25 percent of appraised value would expand the pool of potential home purchasers.

On the question of home mortgage repayment, "mindful of the problems presented on the maturity of short term 'straight' mortgages" the committee advised "to all home buyers the advantages of long term amortized loans" (Gries and Ford 1932, 24). Up to this time, standard mortgages had a three-year term (Weiss 1987, 146). Arguing against this mortgage maturation term, the committee explained that "it has been demonstrated that a long term mortgage, say from 11 to 18 years, that provides amortization of the entire principal [sic], is the most satisfactory to both borrower and lender" (Gries and Ford 1932, 26).

The terms of the standard mortgage loan were mostly the result of the structure of the U.S. banking system. Most U.S. banks and savings institutions were what are known as unit banks. In other words, they had no branches, and operated exclusively out of one office. Throughout the nineteenth century and into the early decades of the twentieth century, branch banking was largely prohibited by the states, or severely limited—such as by only allowing bank branches within the city limits of the home branch (White 1983). By the 1920s branch banking was in greater practice, but it was still limited as twenty-two states forbade bank branches and another nineteen placed varying degrees of restrictions on them. Even in California, where branch banking was politically well established, in 1923 unit banks were successful in having the state superintendent of banks review the opening of new branch offices (White 1983, 163). With savings and deposits fragmented throughout a national system of individual banks operating out of one office, most banks and savings and loans could not afford to have their capital tied up in long-term home loans. In other words, the vast bulk of banks and other savings institutions were simply too undercapitalized to have their assets vested in multi-decade home loans. Hence, the mortgage terms of 60 to 40 percent loaned on appraised value, with a three-year maturity period.

These standard mortgage terms tended to create instability in residential real estate markets. As already noted, high down payments constricted the pool of potential home purchasers. More importantly, relatively short maturation loan terms could work to adversely affect housing markets. While such loans were often renewed, short mortgage terms could serve to depress a real estate market if a local bank needed to increase its liquidity. Since most banks only made direct loans in their community (Zimmerman 1959, 3), a bank that was threatened with insolvency could call in a significant number of its home loans in a community to shore up its finances. Such activity could lead to a number of defaults in a particular area, and/or force many homeowners to prematurely place their homes up for sale. Additionally, if a significant number of homeowners served by a community bank suspected that the bank was not going to renew their mortgage, they were liable to seek to sell. Finally, if bankers sensed a drop in the real estate market in a particular locality they had the option not to renew mortgages in that locality or to ask for higher down payments upon renewal. Logically, in the context of the worsening economic conditions of the Depression (Wicker 1996) the inherent instabilities embedded in the standard lending and home purchasing practices of the period were exacerbated. The committee report noted that "in some states . . . [it was] found that mutual savings banks made their loans for one year, or payable on demand" (Gries and Ford 1932, 26).

Therefore, it was concluded that the longer loan amortization period called for by the Committee on Finance would serve to stabilize the residential real estate market nationally, and make such real estate a more reliable and profitable commodity in which to place investment funds. Created in 1934, the Federal Housing Authority (the unofficial name of the Federal Housing Administration) instituted a policy whereby the federal government guaranteed home loans. Under this program, home mortgages were underwritten if they required 20 percent down and their maturation period was twenty years. Later, this guarantee was modified to 10 percent and twenty-five years (Weiss 1987, 146).

# THE PRODUCTION OF CONSUMER DURABLES

By the 1920s the United States was leading a revolution in consumer durables, goods that are expected to last at least three years. Economic historian Peter Fearon (1987) notes of the other leading industrial power in the 1920s, Great Britain, that its "economy was retarded by the weight of the old staple industries such as cotton textiles, coal, shipbuilding and iron and steel . . ." He explains that this is "in contrast to the striking advance of the consumer durables sector in America" (48). Thus, the U.S. economy excelled in the production of such commodities as household appliances (Markusen 1985; Atkinson 2004; Field 2006).

The most prominent feature of the consumer durables–geared U.S. industrial base was automobile production. In 1920 U.S. automobile firms produced 1.9 million automobiles, and in 1929 4.4 million. This represented 85 percent of total global automotive production.[1] Fearon explains that "the influence of the automobile [on the U.S. economy] was pervasive." For example, "it provided one of the chief markets for the steel industry and for the manufacturers of glass and tyres" (1987, 55). During much of the 1920s, "nearly 17 percent of the total value of fully and semi-manufactured goods was accounted for by automotive products" (Fearon 1987, 58; also see Bardou et al. 1982; St. Clair 1986; Paterson 2007). It is statistics such as these that prompt economic historian Elliot Rosen (2005) to regard the automotive industry as the "nation's principal industry" by the 1920s (118). Economic historian Maury Klein (2007) adds that "during the 1920s the automobile industry became one of the main pillars of the American economy" (181). Another economic historian, Richard B. Du Boff (1989), notes that "during the 1920s, the [automotive] industry became the nation's leader in manufacturing" (83).

While the productive capacity of automotive manufacturers greatly expanded throughout the 1920s, and automobile production had significant implications for overall industrial activity in the United States, the demand for automobiles fluctuated widely. The overall trend in automotive production during the 1920s was upward, but market downturns caused significant production declines in 1921, 1924, and 1927 (Fearon 1987, 58; also see Thomas 1977; Bardou et al. 1982, ch. 6). Additionally, during earlier depressions automobile output "contracted severely" (Fearon 1987, 58).

During the Great Depression, among industrial producers "the collapse in the motor vehicle sector was especially pronounced." By the end of 1929, "the reduction in automobile output was the greatest in the entire manufacturing sector" (Fearon 1987, 91). Jane Holtz Kay (1998), in her history of the automobile in the United States, *Asphalt Nation*, reports that

> by 1932 half the auto plants in Michigan had closed. The saturation of the car market combined with the Depression shut down one out of three dealers. Within a year after the stock market crash, the number of auto workers had shrunk to 100,000, reflecting and accelerating the dwindling car sales. (196; also see Markusen 1985, 165)

A specific difficulty facing the automobile industry in the 1920s and leading into the Depression Era was that most cities during this period were highly centralized and congested (Rosen 1986; Schultz 1989; Fogelson 2001; Tebeau 2003; Beauregard 2006), and this meant that automobiles were either impractical for a large segment of the U.S. populace and/or not needed because places of employment, as well as goods and services, were within walking distance. Additionally, those neighborhoods that were well outside of city centers were normally close to inexpensive trolley service (Dewees 1970; Foster 1981; McShane 1994; Kay 1998, ch. 8). As a result, automobiles were, mostly, a luxury item; prior to the Depression, automobiles were purchased largely for recreational outings (Flink 1975, 1990; Jakle and Sculle 2008).

The production and marketing strategies of most automobile firms during the first two decades of twentieth century reflected the fact that for most the automobile was a luxury. Historian Donald Davis (1988) outlines the production activities of early automotive manufacturers. He points out that most of them produced automobiles that emphasized aesthetics, amenities, and engine power. Hence, they generally shunned the low-end automotive market, wherein automobiles were primarily built for utility, and aesthetic considerations and amenities were not prioritized. Davis argues that automobile manufacturers during the early part of the century tended to produce more expensive automobiles because Detroit's early automotive elite came from a mostly upper-class background and wanted to make automobiles that were commensurate with their class position. By pursuing the middle and upper price range of the automotive market, however, the manufacturers were competing for suburban consumers whose homes could most readily accommodate an automobile and who would be the most likely to use such a commodity. Such consumers belonged predominately to the middle and upper class (Jackson 1985; Fishman 1987; Bruegmann 2005; Fogelson 2005; Kruse and Sugrue 2006). Therefore, suburban consumers made up the most lucrative and stable segment of the automobile market.

Among the early automotive producers, the exception was Henry Ford. Unlike other automobile manufacturers, Ford's primary goal was to build an automobile that maximized utility and was as inexpensive as possible, and he stuck to this goal (Flink 1975, 1990; Davis 1988). Significantly, Ford did not necessarily have a specific consumer in mind when he built his low-end automobile. One of his early partners quoted him as saying in 1916 that "you need not fear about the market, the people will buy them all right, because when you get to making them in quantities, you can make them cheaper, and . . . the market will take care of itself" (as quoted in Davis 1988, 117; ellipsis in original). To the extent that Ford thought about who was the likely consumer for his product it was not urban or suburban dwellers, but farmers (Davis 1988, 121).

One factor that allowed Ford's low-cost automobile strategy to succeed was the fact that by the 1920s urban land developers were building homes away from city centers and trolley lines, and, instead, around the automobile. This was outlined in the last chapter. As a result, automobiles soon became less a luxury item than a necessity.

This was most evident in the case of Los Angeles, where, as described in the last chapter, land developers were particularly aggressive in building entire communities predicated on their residents' automobile ownership. As a result, by the end of the 1920s, the Los Angeles area had become the U.S. region most adapted to the automobile, whereby "residents of Los Angeles purchased more automobiles per capita than did residents of any other city in the country." During this period "there were two automobiles for every five residents in Los Angeles, compared to one for every four residents in Detroit, the next most 'automobile oriented' American city" (Foster 1975, 483). Historians of Los Angeles take these statistics to assume a particular affinity among the city's residents for the automobile (e.g., Fogelson 1967; Foster 1975; Bottles 1987). A more likely cause, however, for the relatively high level of automobile ownership in Los Angeles is that much of the new affordable housing stock was being constructed in areas only accessible by automobile. Moreover, as businesses responded to the increasing mobility of suburban residents, employment, retail outlets, and services were increasingly offered away from the city center and areas serviced by trolleys (Fogelson 1967, 2001; Foster 1975; Wachs 1984; Marchand 1986; Hise 1997, 2001). This created further incentives for Los Angeles residents to obtain an automobile.

Beginning in the mid-1930s, the federal government sponsored the outward development of urban areas, thus making the automobile a necessity for greater numbers of people. Moreover, the horizontal expansion of cities pushed up demand for other consumer durables, such as household appliances (Brenner 2002; Beauregard 2006), because this expansion brought with it larger homes that necessitated more consumer durables to fill such homes.

## THE FEDERAL GOVERNMENT'S PROMOTION OF URBAN SPRAWL

As noted earlier, the federal government, beginning in the mid-1930s, initiated a program to underwrite home mortgages. It did so through the Federal Housing Authority (FHA), whose legislated authority is found in the National Housing Act of 1934. The committee that composed this act was headed by Marriner Eccles, a wealthy Utah businessperson who was an official in the Treasury Department. Also on this five-person committee was

Albert Deane, executive "assistant to the president" of General Motors, Alfred Sloan (Hyman 1976, 144). Eccles's committee was actually a subcommittee of the President's Emergency Committee on Housing. The president's committee included W. Averell Harriman, who was asked to participate because of "his national standing as a businessman" (Hyman 1976, 142; also see Abramson 1992). As historian Sydney Hyman explains, "When the terms of the new housing program were finally agreed to, [Harriman] was expected to 'sell' the program to . . . the business community at large" (1976, 142). Also on the President's Emergency Committee on Housing was John Fahey, chairman of the Federal Home Loan Bank Board (Hyman 1976, 142).[2]

The presence of Sloan (through his assistant) on a presidential housing committee is noteworthy. By this time General Motors was selling one-half of all automobiles in the United States. Beginning in the first decade of the twentieth century automobile firms promoted the reorganization of the nation's transportation infrastructure, spurring automobile dependency. In 1903 automobile manufacturers were supporting the American Road Builders Association and the national movement to have governments at all levels pay for roads and highways that could accommodate automobiles (Paxson 1946, 239–41). In 1911 the American Automobile Association sponsored the first American Roads Congress (American Road Congress 1911). At this congress, Hugh Chalmers (1911), president of the Chalmers Motor Company, conceded that "the automobile industry is, of course, in favor of good roads and would be greatly benefitted by them," but he went on to stress that "since the roads are for all the people, they should be built by all the people, or all the people should contribute to the building of them" (142–43). Chalmers concluded his speech by arguing:

> I believe when the people are thoroughly aroused on this question [of the quality of the U.S. road system] and realize that the benefits of [good roads] are not for one class of people alone, but for all the people alike, that they will rise up some day and demand of the national Congress, to start with, and the State assemblies, in the second place, that they cooperate to the end that we keep pace in road improvement with all other transportation improvements of this century. (149)

Automobile manufacturers were not the only supporters of a national system of automobile-friendly roads and highways. Frederic Paxson (1946), a historian of the U.S. highway movement, notes that many early highway "proposals had money behind them, for chambers of commerce, automobile associations, and industrial organizations" contributed politically to their fruition (242; also see Gonzalez 2005a, ch. 4). Nevertheless, automobile firms were persistently aggressive in promoting automobile-dependent infrastructure (i.e., roads and highways) (Dunn 1998). In the early 1930s, for example, when cash-strapped states began using their gasoline taxes for programs other than road building, "General Motors banded two thousand groups into the National Highway Users Conference to lobby against the practice" (Kay 1998, 205). This lobbying effort yielded the Hayden-Cartwright law of 1934, which determined that "states which diverted the [gasoline] tax to other than road use should be penalized by a reduction in their share of federal aid" (Paxson 1946, 250). Stan Luger, author of *Corporate Power, American Democracy, and the Automobile Industry*, explains that at the 1939 World's Fair General Motors "presented a model of the future based on suburbs and highways" (2005, 174; also see Kay 1998, 218–19). Finally, numerous automotive-related companies, among them General Motors, Standard Oil of California, and Firestone Tire and Rubber, were found by a federal grand jury to have successfully conspired to dismantle electric streetcar (trolley) systems in forty-five U.S. cities, including Los Angeles, San Francisco, and New York during the 1940s (Snell 1974; Yago 1984, ch. 4; Bottles 1987).

Marriner Eccles's biographer (drawing from extensive interviews with Eccles) outlines the thinking underlying the formulation of the National Housing Act of 1934. "A program of new home construction, launched on an adequate scale, would not only gradually provide employment for building trade workers but," more importantly, "accelerate the forward movement of the economy as a whole." It was anticipated that

> its benefits would extend to everyone, from the manufacturers of lace curtains to the manufacturers of lumber, bricks, furniture, cement and electrical appliances. Transportation of supplies would stimulate railroad activity, while the needs generated for the steel rails and rolling stock would have spin-off effects on steel mills. (Hyman 1976, 141)

Moreover, "if banks with excess reserves made loans for home construction, the effect would be to create the basis for new money" (Hyman 1976, 143). Therefore, the purposes of the legislation that authorized the FHA were seemingly to spur consumption, including that of consumer durables, and to prompt the profitable movement of capital out of banks and into the housing sector. Urban sprawl would presumably help accomplish these goals since by the 1920s suburban developers had already demonstrated a predilection for building large, relatively expensive homes on undeveloped tracts of land, far from trolley lines (Stilgoe 1985; Fishman 1987; Weiss 1987; Bruegmann 2005; Fogelson 2005).[3]

Upon its creation, the FHA was placed under stewardship of prominent officials from the real estate sector, and they used their authority to promote the horizontal growth of urban American. Created in 1934,

> FHA's staff was recruited almost entirely from the private sector. Many were corporate executives from a variety of different fields, but real estate and financial backgrounds predominated. For example, Ayers DuBois, who had been a state director of the California Real Estate Association, was an assistant director of FHA's Underwriting Division. Fred Marlow, a well-known Los Angeles subdivider, headed FHA's southern California district office, which led the nation in insuring home mortgages. National figures associated with NAREB, such as real estate economist Ernest Fisher and appraiser Frederick Babcock, directed FHA operations in economics and in underwriting. (Weiss 1987, 146) [Significant for this discussion is the fact that the first administrator of the FHA was an executive from Standard Oil. Also among the FHA's initial leaders were two individuals from the automotive sector: Albert Deane of General Motors [was Deputy Administrator of the FHA] and Ward M. Canaday, "president of the U.S. Advertising Corporation Toledo, with a reputation for sales promotion in the automobile industry." Canaday was the FHA's director of public relations (Zimmerman 1959, 7–8.]

Jeffrey Hornstein (2005), a historian of the U.S. real estate industry, notes that the industry generally "welcomed the FHA . . . both because it promised greatly enhanced general demand for housing and because the agency was run largely by Realtors and their allies in the banking world" (150).

As a way to encourage housing sales, the FHA underwrote home purchases. As explained earlier, it would guarantee 80 percent of home mortgages for qualified homes and buyers for a twenty-year term. (Later, this guarantee was modified to 90 percent and twenty-five years.) Until this time, standard mortgages covered about 50 percent of the home purchase price and had a three-year term (Weiss 1987, 146).

This program gave the FHA the ability to influence the types of homes purchased and, consequently, housing development patterns. Weiss notes:

> Because FHA could refuse to insure mortgages on properties due to their location in neighborhoods that were too poorly planned or unprotected and therefore too "high-risk," it definitely behooved most reputable subdividers to conform to FHA standards. This put FHA officials in the enviable position, far more than any regulatory planning agency, of being able to tell subdividers how to develop their land. (148)

With this power, the FHA promoted the building of large-scale housing developments in outlying areas. Weiss (1987) explains that the Federal Housing "Administration's clear preference . . . was to use conditional commitments [for loan guarantees] specifically to encourage large-scale producers of complete new residential subdivisions, or 'neighborhood units.'" Thus, the FHA, through its loan program, encouraged and subsidized "privately controlled and coordinated development of whole residential communities of predominately single-family housing on the urban periphery" (147) (also see Hornstein 2005, 150–52).

With federal housing policy firmly under the control of the FHA, Kay (1998) writes that it "decentralized housing out of the city and did little to help slum dwellers." In his comprehensive analysis of U.S. suburban development, geographer Peter O. Muller (1981) explains that "the nearly complete suburbanization of the [urban middle class] by the end of the interwar era . . . was greatly accelerated by government policies . . . the most important being the home loan insurance programs launched by the Federal Housing Administration in 1934" (44). Kay (1998) adds:

> Cities remained the center of Depression malaise and neglect. Their expansion ceased or declined compared to suburbs. Twenty-five percent of Detroit's growth was on its periphery, only 3 percent within the city. Likewise, Chicago's suburbs swelled 11 percent, the downtown less than 1 percent. Vast acreage in the central business districts fell for parking spaces. (201)

Kenneth Jackson (1985), in his important history on the suburbanization of urban development in the United States, concurs with Muller's, Weiss's, and Kay's assessments of the bias within the FHA for new housing stock in outlying areas. Jackson (1985) writes that "in practice, FHA insurance went to new residential developments on the edges of metropolitan areas, to the neglect of core cities" (206). As a result, Jackson notes that between the years 1942 and 1968 the "FHA had a vast influence on the suburbanization of the United States" (209).

By promoting low-density urban development and sprawl, the federal government eschewed a network of intellectuals advocating what was known as *social housing* during the 1920s and 1930s. Drawing from experiences in Europe, such thinkers argued that apartment complex housing that emphasized community living—wherein services such as day care and schooling for children were provided, as well as recreational facilities and activities—was economically and socially preferable to suburban tract housing (Radford 1996). Historian Gail Radford (1996) points out that the few U.S. experiments in social housing proved to be successful. These projects, built in the 1930s in places such as Philadelphia and Harlem, were well planned, affordable, aesthetically pleasing, and provided important amenities to its residents. Moreover, Radford finds that residents of U.S. social housing generally found living there to be agreeable and advantageous. While federal housing projects built in the post–World War II period only allowed the poor (Bloom 2008), the housing reformers' experiments were mostly occupied by white and blue collar workers.

## URBAN SPRAWL AND THE CONSUMPTION OF CONSUMER DURABLES

In her historical analysis of U.S. consumption patterns, economic historian Martha L. Olney finds that

> between 1919 and 1928, [U.S. households] spent annually an average of $267 each on durable goods—$172 for major durables (now mostly automobiles and parts rather than furniture) and only $96 for minor durables (still mostly china and tableware, house furnishings, and jewelry and watches). (1991, 9; parentheses in original)

After a number of decades of horizontal urban growth (Muller 1981; Cohen 2003; Bruegmann 2005; Lassiter 2005; Beauregard 2006), by 1979–86, households annually spent an average of $3,271 each for durable goods, with $2,230 for major durables (still predominantly automobiles and parts) and $1,041 for minor durable goods (now house furnishings, miscellaneous other durable goods, and jewelry and watches) (1991, 9). Conveyed in constant dollars, households between 1919 and 1928 spent an average of $955 on consumer durables, and $3,353 between 1979 and 1986 (Olney 1991, 9). Olney adds that "strong growth purchases of automobiles and parts remains evident: average annual purchases for 1919–28 were four times greater than the average for 1909–18, and growth continued through the post–World War II years." Additionally, "purchases of household appliances and the 'entertainment complexes'—radios, televisions, pianos, and other musical instruments—showed a similar pattern" (1991, 22).

Utilizing statistical analysis, Olney (1991) demonstrates that the dramatic increases in the consumption of durable goods exceeded overall increases in income during the pre–Depression Era and the post–World War II periods. It is for this reason that Olney contends that the 1920s marks the beginning of the consumer durables revolution in the United States. She attributes the surges in the consumption of consumer durables to two factors: advertising and the availability of consumer credit. She acknowledges, however, that advertising (also see Miller 1991; Visor 2001; Dawson 2003;

and Henthorn 2006), and especially consumer credit (also see Calder 1999; Gelpi and Julie-Labruyère 2000, ch. 8; Olegario 2006), were not as widespread during the 1920s as they were after World War II.[4] What was evident during both of these periods was an increasing trend of urban sprawl, expanding demand for consumer durables

Today, U.S. urban sprawl has international economic ramifications. The United States is the world's largest consumer (French 1997; Brenner 2002, 2004; Frumkin 2004; Uchitelle 2006). U.S. consumers, excluding government and businesses, purchase close to 20 percent of the world's total economic output (Goodman 2007). Importantly, European, Japanese, and South Korean automakers count heavily on access to the huge U.S. automobile market to attain profitability. With one-third less population than Western and Central Europe, the United States consumes, on average, two million more automobiles annually (during peak years: fifteen million versus seventeen million), and, at least until recently, one-half of all automobiles purchased in the United States were of the highly profitable SUV and light truck varieties (Bradsher 2002; Conybeare 2004; Becker 2006, 12; Bunkley 2008 August 12; Boudette and Norihiko 2008). The Japanese automakers Honda and Toyota (the world's second-largest automobile manufacturer), for instance, derive two-thirds of their overall profits from sales in the United States (Zaun 2005; Fackler 2006). It is also noteworthy that General Motors, the world's largest manufacturer of automobiles, registers over 40 percent of its sales in the U.S. market (Bunkley 2008 Jan. 24). (The United States contains about 4.5 percent of the world's population.)

## CONCLUSION

The development of urban sprawl in the United States is consistent with the economic elite approach to public policy formation. This becomes evident through historical analysis. As explained in chapter 3, the techniques of sprawl were developed and promoted during the early part of the twentieth century by leading homebuilders and adopted throughout the U.S. real estate industry. Beyond the real estate industry, economic elites in the early 1930s embraced urban sprawl—more explicitly, home construction pushing up demand for capital and consumer durables—as the way to absorb excess capital and the productive output of the U.S. industrial base. The U.S. industrial base was geared toward the production of consumer durables—most importantly, automobiles. The support by economic elites for urban sprawl is apparent in both the Committee on Finance of the President's Conference on Home Building and Home Ownership, and the President's Emergency Committee on Housing. The latter was directly responsible for the formulation of National Housing Act of 1934, which led to the creation of the Federal Housing Authority (FHA). Early policymakers within the FHA were largely from the real estate sector. Subsequently, the FHA put forward the key impetus underlying the sprawling of U.S. urban growth.

Pointing to Olney's instructive work, we can see that consumer durables consumption in the United States took off during the 1920s, and, again, throughout the post–World War II period (also see Brenner 2002 and Beauregard 2006). Olney suggests that advertising and consumer credit can account for this consumer durables revolution. Advertising and especially consumer credit, however, were nascent in the 1920s; urban sprawl, which burgeoned in the 1920s (and was nationally institutionalized in the postwar period) can better account for the U.S. consumer durables revolution. Urban sprawl in the United States, and the consumer durables revolution that sprawl seemingly spawned, were made possible by ample stocks of oil. It is to this issue that I turn next.

# Chapter Five

# U.S. Oil Policy and Urban Sprawl

The principal strategic considerations that governed U.S. oil policy in the post–World War II period revolved around competition with the Soviet Union (i.e., the cold war) and obtaining sufficient petroleum supplies for the relatively high U.S. demand. The former tended to be the more prominent consideration throughout the 1950s and 1960s, as there existed a significant surplus of petroleum on the world market and, as a result, U.S. petroleum consumption levels were seemingly a non-issue. In the aftermath of the oil shocks of the 1970s, however, U.S. oil policy centered on ensuring enough supply to maintain U.S. consumption levels. As a result, the Middle East took on greater importance because it became patently evident that U.S. consumption levels could not continue without the oil from this region.

Hence, federal energy policy has historically been liberal when it comes to consumption. In other words, such policy has not sought to curb consumption, nor generally sought to change consumption patterns to sources that are more secure and/or abundant. This liberal policy persisted even when it became clear that increasing oil dependence was a severe geopolitical and economic liability. On the supply side, U.S. oil policy has been geared toward maintaining prices whereby consumption can continue unabated. These policies are consistent with the overall argument for this book—namely, that urban sprawl in the United States is a requisite feature of modern global capitalism. Inexpensive energy inputs, especially cheap petroleum, are required to sustain urban sprawl. The outlines and trajectory of U.S. oil policy have historically been set by economic elites.

## PETROLEUM AND THE COLD WAR

Foreign policy planning in the United States for the post–World War II period was conducted by the Council on Foreign Relations (CFR). During the war the State Department did not have the resources necessary to devote to policy planning for the postwar period. So, drawing on a grant from the Rockefeller Foundation (Parmar 2002b), the CFR became the primary organization planning for the time when the war would end, and in this planning effort it collaborated closely with the Department of State.

Since its inception in 1921 the CFR has been an economic elite–led policy discussion group designed to treat questions of foreign affairs (Shoup and Minter 1977; Domhoff 1990, ch. 5). During its early history the CFR received significant financial contributions from Chase National Bank, Standard Oil of New Jersey, IBM, General Motors, General Electric, Texaco, and the National City Bank of New York (Shoup 1974, 42). Inderjeet Parmar, who has written extensively on the CFR (1995, 1999, 2004), describes in the following the corporate director positions held by the fifty-five CFR directors for the years 1921–1946:

> The fifty-five leaders held at least seventy-four corporate director-ships. . . . The corporations concerned were among the largest in the United States: Myron C. Taylor of U.S. Steel and AT&T; Leon Fraser, Owen D. Young and Philip D. Reed of General Electric; Clarence M. Wooley and Lewis W. Douglas of General Motors; R.C. Leffingwell of J.P. Morgan and Co.; and Frank Polk, Doug-las, John H. Finley, David F. Houston, and Reed of Mutual Life Insurance Company of New York. (1995, 82)

Reflective of the elite social standing of CFR directors during this period, the fifty-five directors in Parmar's (1995) study "held, on average, at least three [elite social club] memberships, with the Cosmos and Metropolitan clubs in Washington, DC, and Century and Knickerbockers of New York, being the most popular. In all, 170 club memberships were reported" (82).

The involvement of the CFR in setting the trajectory for U.S. post-war foreign policy has been thoroughly documented and discussed (Notter 1949 [1975]; Shoup 1974; Shoup and Minter 1977; Schulzinger 1984; Domhoff 1990, ch. 5; Parmar 1995, 1999, 2004; Smith 2003). As Parmar (1995) notes, "From 1939 onwards, the Council, in collaboration with the State Department, established the War and Peace Studies Project, the aim of which was to outline the national interests of the USA as a basis for official planning for a post-war foreign policy" (83). Geographer Neil Smith observes that the CFR's War and Peace Studies project "established a vital foundation for State Department postwar planning" (2003, 331).

The key policy principle put forward by the CFR in its War and Peace Studies project was the "Grand Area" concept. The basic idea was that the United States needed a "Grand Area" of the globe "in order for its econ-omy to function without fundamentally changing" (Parmar 1995, 83).

When proposed in 1942, this vital area was to comprise the "Western Hemisphere, Continental Europe and Mediterranean Basin (excluding Russia), the Pacific Area and the Far East, and the British Empire (excluding Canada)" (Shoup 1974, 109). The CFR advised that "to integrate the Grand Area, the United States was to develop institutions for international financial collaboration; for international monetary exchange; to resolve raw materials problems; and so on" (Parmar 1995, 83).

These policy prescriptions would in the main presage U.S. foreign policy throughout the cold war. Most importantly, the Grand Area concept became embodied in U.S. containment policy. This policy sought to limit the Soviet bloc within its post–World War II boundaries, with the expectation that by hemming in the Soviet Union and its satellites the West would undermine their long-term economic and political viability. While put forward as an assertive policy directed at the Soviet Union (albeit not a militarily confrontational one), U.S. containment policy sought to keep the global area viewed as necessary by the CFR for the functioning of the U.S. market economy within the Western allies' sphere of influence (Domhoff 1990, ch. 5). In this way, containment policy allowed the West to regain and maintain its economic dynamism, while seeking to stifle that of the Soviet bloc.

Significant for this discussion is that within the Grand Area laid out by the CFR in its War and Peace Study were all the known major oil-bearing regions outside of the Soviet Union. A vice president for Chase National Bank opined in a letter to a high-ranking State Department official in 1943, "The future of the post-war world is dependent upon the disposition made of petroleum as an economic and social force" (as quoted in Randall 2005, 135). In the Western Hemisphere, the United States, Canada, Venezuela, and Mexico had been major oil producers before World War II. Elsewhere, Royal Dutch/Shell since the late nineteenth century had drawn its key oil supplies from the Dutch East Indies, and heading into World War II the British sphere of influence had included Iraq, Kuwait, Iran, and Saudi Arabia. By the late 1930s all of these countries were known to contain substantial reserves of petroleum (Yergin 1991). U.S. foreign policy from the end of World War II was strongly geared toward keeping these countries/regions as allies/protectorates (Shaffer 1983; Painter 1986; Bromley 1991; Rutledge 2005), like the rest of the CFR's proposed Grand Area (e.g., the Korean and Vietnam Wars) (Krasner 1978; Layne 2006).

## U.S. OIL POLICY

In 1973 the Persian Gulf region of the Middle East, however, took on particular importance for the Western allies. What came into relief in 1973 is that the region contained the key supplies of petroleum for the Western world. The petroleum-bearing countries of the region are Bahrain, Iran, Iraq, Kuwait, Saudi Arabia, United Arab Emirates, and Qatar; together they possess the majority of the world's known petroleum reserves, with Saudi Arabia alone estimated to hold 25 percent (Parra 2004; Blatt 2005, 100; Nersesian 2007, 205; Duffield 2008).

The Persian Gulf's strategic importance is in significant part the result of U.S. oil policies. This is particularly apparent on the demand side. As U.S. cities became more and more sprawled (Muller 1981; Beauregard 2006), and as a result more automobile-dependent (Foster 1981; Kenworthy and Laube 1999), U.S. oil consumption steadily climbed (Blair 1976; Shaffer 1983; Philip 1994; Rutledge 2005). Between 1946 and 1953, for instance, gasoline usage went from thirty billion gallons annually to forty-nine billion, amounting to a yearly growth rate of slightly over 7.2 percent. By 1958 U.S. gasoline consumption exceeded fifty-nine billion gallons (American Petroleum Institute 1959, 246–47).

Eventually, U.S. consumption had a detrimental effect on its own oil production. This was important because the United States had historically been capable of reducing world petroleum prices by increasing its own production. By 1970, however, U.S. oil production had peaked, and could no longer be used to regulate world prices (Yergin 1991; Deffeyes 2001). When Saudi Arabia imposed a selective embargo on countries favorable to Israel in 1973, the United States was importing close to 40 percent of its oil needs, and could not respond to the shortfall created by the embargo with domestic production (Blair 1976; Shaffer 1983; Vietor 1984; Philip 1994; Rutledge 2005; Bronson 2006).

U.S. policymakers had made little effort to ensure that sufficient domestic stocks of oil would be available in case the country lost access to foreign reserves. This failure is reflected in the Petroleum Reserve Corporation plan. Additionally, U.S. oil import quotas actually encouraged the depletion of U.S. reserves instead of drawing on foreign supplies.

## THE PETROLEUM RESERVE CORPORATION

During World War II a plan was posited to conserve U.S. oil supplies. Consistent with state autonomy theory, it was initiated within the government. Its leading champion was Harold Ickes, the Secretary of the Interior. The plan called for the establishment of a government corporation, the Petroleum Reserve Corporation (PRC), that would participate directly in U.S. petroleum operations in Saudi Arabia (Stoff 1980, ch. 3; Randall 2005, ch. 6). At that time the companies heading oil operations in Saudi Arabia were the Texas Company (later Texaco) and Standard Oil of California (later Chevron). They operated through a subsidiary, the California Arabian Standard Oil Company (Aramco in 1944). The idea underlying Ickes's plan was that a government-managed California Arabian Company could direct Saudi oil to the United States, thereby easing demand for U.S. supplies. Two admirals who supported the creation of the PRC and its partial takeover of California Arabian held that it would allow the United States to "build in" its petroleum reserves (as quoted in Randall 2005, 140). In advocating for the PRC plan, the undersecretary for the Navy, William Bullitt, was explicit in his reasoning when he wrote to President Roosevelt that the U.S. "domestic reserve should be kept in the ground as a strategic reserve and that our current needs should be filled from sources of oil outside the continental limits of the United States" (Bullitt 1943, 6).

Supporters of the PRC plan argued that it would help the United States avoid the type of petroleum shortfall that it would ultimately experience in 1973 (Stoff 1980, ch. 3; Randall 2005, ch. 6). Bullitt, for one, held in 1943 that even at peacetime extraction rates U.S. oil reserves would be exhausted in fourteen years (1943, 3). Wartime petroleum extraction piqued concerns about the viability of U.S. supplies and its oil security, as the United States provided close to six billion of the almost seven billion barrels of crude used by the allies from 1941 to 1945 (Jacoby 1974, 37).

There was an important historical precedent for such government ownership and involvement in an oil concern. In 1914, the British government had become the majority partner in the Anglo-Persian Oil Company (later British Petroleum [BP]). Anglo-Persian was in need of funds to continue oil exploration in Iran, and the British government wanted direct control over a company that managed substantial supplies of petroleum, as British naval ships at the time were being converted from coal to oil use. With its investment the government acquired 51 percent ownership of Anglo-Persian (Ferrier 1982).

President Roosevelt endorsed the Ickes-backed plan, and in July 1943 an executive order created the PRC. The PRC's board of directors was composed of the secretaries of State, War, the Navy, and the Interior, and the Director of Economic Warfare ("By-Laws of the Petroleum Reserve Corporation" 1943).

There was strong and seemingly unified oil industry opposition, however, to the planned takeover by the PRC, manifested through two oil industry policy-planning organizations: the Petroleum Administrator for War's (PAW) Foreign Operations Committee, and the Petroleum Industry War Council (PIWC). Stephan J. Randall, a historian of U.S. foreign oil policy, observes that "the Foreign Operations Committee of the PAW expressed accurately the industry viewpoint when it recommended that 'as a general rule, the Government should not become financially interested in any foreign oil operations, either through purchase of stock in companies operating in foreign countries or by acquisition of concessions in foreign countries'" (2005, 144). PAW was a government agency convened for wartime purposes, whose foreign operations committee was composed of "nine industry executives experienced in foreign operations and drawn from the major [oil] companies" (Randall 2005, 117). The Interior Department's Petroleum Industry War Council (PIWC)

> was a larger, more amorphous entity, drawing together more than seventy [petroleum] industry leaders, including the presidents of each of the trade associations within the [petroleum] industry. Its chairman, William R. Boyd, Jr., was also president of the American Petroleum Institute [an oil industry trade association]. (Randall 2005, 118; also see *A Documentary History of the Petroleum Reserve Corporation* 1974, 59–60)

In response to the plans of the PRC, the PIWC passed a resolution categorically stating that "the United States Government should under no circumstances acquire title or ownership or directly or indirectly engage in foreign oil exploration, development or operation" ("Resolutions Adopted by the Petroleum Industry War Council" 1943, 70).

Independent oil producers in the United States also opposed the activities of the PRC, but they may have done so less for ideological reasons than out of self-interest. Increased foreign oil production could serve to push down the domestic price of oil, which would jeopardize domestic oil operations. Therefore, insofar as government investment through the PRC might increase foreign oil production and enable privileged access to the U.S. market, the Independent Petroleum Association staked out a position of opposition to the PRC ("Resolutions Adopted by the Petroleum Industry War Council" 1944, 82–83).

Ultimately, the Texas Company and Standard Oil of California refused to sell any stock in California Arabian to the PRC, and the plan to have the U.S. government become directly involved in foreign oil operations subsequently died, as did the PRC itself in 1944 (Stoff 1980, 80–88; Randall 2005, ch. 6).[1]

The PIWC put forward a different conception of the United States' interest as it related to oil supplies, and advocated specific policy proposals to serve this interest. The PIWC held that oil supplies under the control of U.S. petroleum firms were, for national and economic security purposes, like oil supplies controlled by the U.S. government. A report by PAW's Foreign Operations Committee, entitled "A Foreign Oil Policy for the United States," which was endorsed by PIWC (National Oil Policy Committee 1944, 77), asserted that "*oil in the hands of nationals of the United States is equally available for national security with oil owned or financially shared in by the Government of the United States*" (1943, 63; emphasis in original). In a February 1944 report entitled "A National Oil

Policy for the United States," the PIWC's National Oil Policy Committee rejected any government effort to conserve or manage domestic oil reserves because "*locking up proven reserves by the process of suppression of existing production, or by acquisition of proven oil fields by purchase or condemnation would be harmful to the hope of a continued, vigorous domestic industry*" (National Oil Policy Committee, 74; emphasis in original). In order to bolster the oil security of the United States, the "*Government of the United States should encourage private American enterprise to engage in the development of oil resources abroad*" (Foreign Operations Committee 1943, 63; emphasis in original). Additionally,

> The combined domestic and foreign oil reserves held by nationals of the United States constitute a smaller proportion of the petroleum reserves of the world than the ratio of the United States consumption of petroleum to total world consumption. Action is needed to enlarge the reserves under the stewardship of nationals of the United States. (Foreign Operations Committee 1943, 65)

The Foreign Operations Committee went on to add that "nationals of the United States should not be in a position of inferiority in acquiring and developing petroleum reserves within the territories or spheres of influence of other nations" (1943, 65).

In its February 1944 report, the PIWC's National Oil Policy Committee echoed the Foreign Operations Committee's arguments on oil security when it averred that "*the national security and economic stability of the United States can be greatly enhanced by adequate world oil developments, under the leadership of United States nationals*" (National Oil Policy Committee 1944, 77; emphasis in original). Consistent with the PIWC's and Foreign Operations Committee's recommendations, U.S. foreign oil policy throughout the postwar period was limited to gaining access for U.S. oil firms to sources of petroleum worldwide (Shaffer 1983; Parra 2004; Rutledge 2005; Duffield 2008).

## Oil Import Quotas

From the perspective of U.S. domestic oil producers, this policy was too successful, especially for the independent oil companies, which relied mostly, if not exclusively, on domestic production. Difficulties arose because too much oil was being extracted worldwide, and this was pushing down oil prices to the point that domestic oil production was threatened. By the 1950s most U.S. oil reserves were mature, and the "easy" oil toward the top of reservoirs had already been extracted. Thus, the remaining oil was more expensive to extract, and U.S. oil could not compete with oil extracted from foreign reservoirs, which in many cases had just been tapped. So as surplus oil was entering the global market, producers found it difficult to make a profit on domestic production (Blair 1976, ch. 7; Banks 1980; Deffeyes 2001).

Overproduction had been an issue for the U.S. oil industry almost from its inception. Entry into the oil extraction business in the nineteenth century was relatively easy. Standard Oil came to dominate the oil industry in this era not through extraction, but through petroleum refining. Standard would buy relatively inexpensive crude from producers and charge a premium price on refined petroleum products (Yergin 1991, ch. 2). Overproduction became a more serious problem because of new oil finds. Particularly devastating for the oil industry was a major discovery in east Texas in the early 1930s (Davis 1993, ch. 3; Olien and Olien 2002).

Exacerbating the industry's overproduction problems was the courts' refusal to establish ownership over petroleum reservoirs. As a result, anyone who tapped into a reservoir was permitted to extract as much oil from it as they could, as long as they held legal title to the land on which they had established their well. This served as an anticonservation measure; because no one knew if someone else was extracting petroleum from the same reservoir they were working, the logical course of action was to extract all the oil from their own well as quickly as possible (McDonald 1971; Miller 1973).

In the 1930s state governments put forward "proration" programs in an effort to shore up severely depressed domestic oil prices. Most oil producing states set production targets and then allocated a portion of the target to different producers within their state. In turn, refiners in a state would be limited to refining a portion of this production target. With global foreign oil surpluses being created through foreign production the proration system was faltering by the 1950s, as domestic refiners could augment/replace their domestic oil allotment with inexpensive foreign crude.

To reverse the deteriorating economic position of domestic oil production, the U.S. government imposed an import quota system in 1959, which would stay in place until the oil shock of 1973. While the import quotas contained important loopholes for Mexican and Canadian petroleum, nevertheless the result of the quota system was to maintain/increase extraction of oil from U.S. reserves that could have otherwise been drawn from Middle Eastern and other foreign supplies (Blair 1976, ch. 7; Vietor 1984, ch. 6; Davis 1993, ch. 3).

The major oil companies found the import system advantageous, and there is evidence that they helped bring it about (Blair 1976, 171–75). The majors had significant oil operations in the United States, and this aspect of their companies benefited from rising domestic oil prices. Moreover, major oil firms—e.g., Standard of Jersey (later Exxon), Socony (later Mobil), Standard of California, Texaco, Shell, and Gulf—were given favorable treatment with regard to the oil that was allowed in from outside of North America, to the disadvantage of international independent producers (Shaffer 1983, 125 and 129). Additionally, the oil that international oil companies drew from the Middle East that could not be sold in the United States would be channeled to Europe. Oil companies were under pressure to extract petroleum from Middle Eastern countries in excess of worldwide demand, because in exchange for granting firms oil concessions host governments expected a certain income through petroleum royalties. This excess crude would be directed at European markets where low prices served to establish oil as the primary fuel for industry and home heating, and in the process displace the use of coal for these purposes (Shaffer 1983, ch. 7; Hatch 1986; Haugland et al. 1998, ch. 2).

## THE OIL SHOCKS OF THE 1970s

Therefore, leading up to the oil shocks of the 1970s U.S. oil reserves had been depleted for a number of reasons: wartime exigencies, an underdeveloped legal regime, import quotas, a failure to plan, and high levels of domestic consumption. What is theoretically and historically significant, however, is the response of the U.S. government when the dependency and vulnerability of the U.S. economy on foreign sources of petroleum came into stark relief in 1973. No effort was put forward by the U.S. government to rollback or limit urban sprawl and the automobile dependence that it spawned. The significance of the U.S. response comes into sharp focus particularly when compared to the response of Western European countries to the same oil crises—countries whose governments did not rely on urban sprawl to revive and sustain their economies.

The United States responded militarily to its apparent dependency. U.S. policymakers used the country's superior political and military position to ensure that Persian Gulf oil remained in the U.S. sphere of influence, and that the region's petroleum sufficiently flowed. Until 1979, the United States supplied the Iranian government with military equipment and training sufficient to safeguard the petroleum reserves of the region against Soviet aggression. After its client regime in Iran collapsed (which brought on a second oil crisis), the United States sought to build up its military capabilities in the region, culminating with a direct military presence after the first Persian Gulf war in 1991 (Bill 1988; Ikenberry 1988; Bromley 1991; Yetiv 2004, 2008).

This emphasis on the supply side to deal with the United States' energy problems of the 1970s is reflected in two reports put out by the Twentieth Century Fund (now the Century Fund), a foundation that in the 1950s and 1960s sponsored studies on the natural resource needs of the United States' expanding economy (e.g., Dewhurst et al. 1955; Carskadon and Soule

1957; Barach et al. 1964). In the early 1970s, the Twentieth Century Fund created two policy-planning groups, composed largely of economic elites, that put forward proposals to deal with the petroleum situation. One task force, convened in 1973, was titled "The Twentieth Century Fund Task Force on United States Energy Policy," and included a director and senior vice president of Exxon, a vice chairman of the board of the American Electric Power Company, Walter J. Levy (a consultant to most major oil firms ["As Oil Consultant" 1969; Shaffer 1983, 214–18]),[2] a vice chairman of the board of Texas Commerce Bancshares (a major Texas bank [Buenger and Pratt 1986, 299]), and the chairman of the board of Carbomin International Corporation (an international mining firm). The second task force, formed in 1974, was known as "The Twentieth Century Fund Task Force on the International Oil Crisis." Walter J. Levy and the executives from Carbomin and Texas Commerce Bancshares also served on this task force, as did the chairman of the board of Atlantic Richfield (an oil firm), a managing director of Dillon, Read & Co. (a leading New York investment management firm), the chairman of the board of the Louis Dreyfus Corporation (an investment management firm), the chairman and president of The First National Bank of Chicago, and a consultant to Wells Fargo Bank (a major California bank). Also on these task forces were academics (mostly economists) from Princeton, Harvard, MIT, and the University of Virginia, as well as the presidents of Resources for the Future (which was on the two task forces) and the Carnegie Institution (only on the energy policy group)—both of which are economic elite–led research institutes (Twentieth Century Fund Task Force on the International Oil Crisis 1975, vii–viii; Twentieth Century Fund Task Force on United States Energy Policy 1977, xi–xii; Winks 1997, 44 and 196).

In the wake of the 1973 oil shortage and the Organization of Petroleum Exporting Countries (OPEC) seeking to maintain high oil prices, both of the Twentieth Century Fund's task forces advised that the United States should strive to develop sources of oil and energy outside of the OPEC countries. This would serve to reduce the strategic positioning of OPEC countries over petroleum and petroleum prices. OPEC includes the Persian Gulf oil producers (excluding Bahrain), plus Algeria, Angola, Ecuador, Libya, Nigeria, Venezuela, and (until 2009) Indonesia. The Twentieth Century Fund's task force on the international oil crisis advised that "the best remedy for the problems caused by the increased price of oil [brought about by OPEC members] would be, simply, to lower the price" of petroleum. "The Task Force believes that this remedy should be sought through reliance on market forces" (1975, 9). The task force goes on to explain in its report that *"the most effective means of exerting market pressure will be to accelerate exploration for crude and develop producing capacity from"* areas outside of OPEC (1975, 9; emphasis in original). The task force on U.S. energy policy averred: "*That it is essential that the nation take firm and forceful action to implement a comprehensive near-term energy program designed to assure greater availability of domestic supplies of oil and other sources of energy*" (emphasis in original).

Therefore, the key recommendations put forward by these policy-planning groups, made up in large part of economic elites, in light of U.S. oil dependency on OPEC countries was to expand the supply of available energy free from OPEC control, and not necessarily to reduce energy consumption.

Both of these groups, in their reports, called for greater energy efficiency, or what they labeled in their reports as "conservation." The difficulty is that increased energy efficiency does not necessarily reduce overall consumption levels. The energy policy group, in a section of its report entitled "Measures to Promote Conservation," "*endorse[d] the use of special incentives to encourage further investment in energy-saving capital goods and consumer durables because conserving energy is as important as increasing the supply*" (1975, 23; emphasis in original). It specifically suggested in its report the use of a "luxury" tax to discourage the purchase of large, less efficient automobiles. Moreover, the implementation of "excise taxes levied annually and collected with state registration fees also might serve to encourage quicker scrapping of cars that consume above-average amounts of gasoline" (1977, 23–24). Finally:

> The Task Force favor[ed] the continuation of such energy-conserving measures as reasonable speed limits on highways, building standards that reduce the use of energy for heating and cooling, and requirements that appliances bear tags disclosing their energy-utilization efficiency. (1977, 24)

The task force on the international oil crisis did not set out specific conservation proposals. Instead, it deferred to the energy policy task force on this (1975, 15).

Increased energy efficiency can lead to overall lower levels of petroleum consumption. Energy savings from increased efficiency, however, can be offset by increased economic growth ("Energy Efficiency Fails to Cut Consumption" 2007; Herring and Sorrell 2009). This is especially the case within sprawled urban regions, where greater levels of economic activity can lead to a larger workforce driving to and from work, and increased demand for spacious homes on the urban periphery. So whereas automobiles may become more fuel efficient, in the context of diffusely organized cities more automobiles and longer driving distances can lead to greater overall gasoline/oil consumption—in spite of gains made in fuel efficiency (Harrington and McConnell 2003, ch. 6 and 7). This is precisely what has transpired in the United States. The current U.S. automobile fleet is more efficient than the U.S. automobile fleet of the early 1970s (Energy Information Administration 2004, 57); however, because of a substantially enlarged automobile population and ever-increasing amounts of driving, gasoline/diesel consumption in the United States today substantially exceeds that of the 1970s. According to energy economist Ian Rutledge (2005), in 1970 automobiles in the United States consumed 7.1 million barrels per day of petroleum, whereas by 2001 that figure increased to 10.1 million (10). Today, according to government agencies, automobile driving in the United States consumes more than 10 percent of total global oil production.[3]

Largely because of the steady growth of gasoline/diesel consumption in the United States (Duffield 2008, ch. 2), its economy consumes about 25 percent of the world's total petroleum production (with less than 5 percent of the global population).[4] This is especially glaring because in the aftermath of the spike in oil prices in the 1970s, U.S. factories and utilities shifted from petroleum-based fuels to other sources of energy (mostly, coal, natural gas, and nuclear power) (Philip 1994, 195; Roberts 2004; Rutledge 2005, ch. 1; Wald 2005; Podobnik 2006, ch. 5 and 6; Duffield 2008, ch. 2).

It is telling that neither of the Twentieth Century Fund's task forces counseled less driving, or mass transportation, as conservation measures to counter OPEC price strategies. Such a recommendation would have called attention to urban sprawl and the automobile dependence that it creates as political issues.

# EUROPEAN POST–WORLD WAR II OIL POLICIES

The advanced industrialized countries of the Federal German Republic (i.e., West Germany) and France, which had little appreciable domestic oil production, responded to the petroleum crises of the 1970s by trying to severely limit their use of oil. Due to major oil strikes in 1966 along its northern coast, Great Britain had less immediate need to reduce its oil use. Overall, the nations of Western Europe had not developed the petroleum vulnerability that the United States had by the 1970s. This is particularly because urban zones in these countries were not as sprawled and automobile dependent as in the United States (Kenworthy and Laube 1999).

Postwar Western European concerns about energy security were manifest in the 1955 Armand report and the 1956 Hartley report, both sponsored by Council of Ministers of the Organization for European Economic Cooperation (OEEC). Primarily because of fear over trade imbalances, the Armand report (1955), entitled *Some Aspects of the European Energy Problem: Suggestions for Collective Action* and named after its author

Louis Armand (a French government official), advised against dependency on foreign sources of oil. Instead, Armand advised Western European countries to rely on domestic sources of energy, on sources of energy in Europe's African colonies, and especially on nuclear power.

Shortly after receiving the Armand report, the OEEC created a Commission for Energy. The commission sponsored what became known as the Hartley report, named after its chairperson Harold Hartley of Great Britain. The authors of this report extended their concerns over oil imports beyond trade imbalance issues, and expressed fears about oil security. According to the Hartley report, "[T]here are inevitable risks in the increasing dependence on Western Europe on outside [oil] supplies, particularly when most of them must come from one small area of the world" (i.e., the Persian Gulf) (Commission for Energy 1956, 25). Accordingly, the report recommended that by 1975 Western Europe should draw only 20 to 33 percent of its energy from imported petroleum, and the rest predominately from coal (Commission for Energy 1956, 73). The Hartley report authors averred that "coal must remain the mainstay of the Western European energy economy" (Commission for Energy 1956, 26), recommending that Western European domestic coal production satisfy half of the region's energy needs, with the rest satisfied by hydro-power, natural gas, oil, imported coal, and nuclear energy (Commission for Energy 1956, 73).

Both the Hartley and Armand reports counseled that Western European governments should intervene to ensure the region's energy stability. The Hartley commission suggested that

> in order to deal effectively with the urgent problems involved in the supply and demand of energy, each Member country will require an energy policy suited to its own circumstances and its needs and resources. This policy should include some measure of coordination between the different forms of energy. (Commission on Energy 1956, 56)

Armand held that OEEC countries should avoid "a situation in which competition between the various forms of energy acts to the detriment of the community as a whole" (1955, 46).

Subsequent to the Armand and Hartley reports, the OEEC formed the Energy Advisory Commission, chaired by Professor Austin Robinson. In 1960 this commission put forward a new report on European energy, entitled *Towards a New Energy Pattern in Europe*. Unlike the Armand or Hartley reports, which had advocated government promotion of domestic coal (Hartley) or nuclear power (Armand) in order to limit imported oil use, the Robinson Commission argued that Western Europe should rely on inexpensive imported petroleum for much of its energy needs. As to the security of oil supplies, new discoveries in Venezuela, West Africa, and Libya, and "in particular, discoveries of oil and natural gas in the Sahara [e.g., Algeria] have created new possibilities of important supplies in an area more closely integrated into the economy of Western Europe." Therefore, "as a result, there has been made possible a wider diversification of oil supplies to Western Europe" (Energy Advisory Commission 1960, 13–14). The Robinson energy commission went on to argue that "it does not seem likely that shortages of oil or other supplies will make themselves felt in acute form by 1975" (1960, 83). With regard to the region's balance of payments, the commission asserted that "if Western Europe can maintain its share of world markets for manufactures, the import of the increased proportions of the total supplies of energy that have emerged from our study may reasonably be expected to be within the probable limits of its capacity" (1960, 61). The way to cover the costs of imported energy was to maintain or expand Western Europe's world market share of industrial products. A key means to do this is to keep the cost of energy inputs low. Thus, "When formulating a long-term energy policy, the paramount consideration should be a plentiful supply of low-cost energy." Additionally, "the general interest is best served by placing the least possible obstacles in the way of economic development of the newer and cheaper sources of energy" (Energy Advisory Commission 1960, 83–84). In other words, Western European governments should not subsidize nuclear power or coal to the detriment of abundant and inexpensive petroleum supplies.

Especially in the areas of electricity and industrial production, as well as home heating, Western European countries did pursue the more liberal course advocated by the Robinson Commission. As a result, by the early 1970s 60 percent of this region's energy needs were met through imported oil (Shaffer 1983, ch. 7; Haugland et al. 1998, 55). In the case of automobile transportation, however, Western European countries have historically instituted more restrictive policies. Haugland and his associates, experts on European energy, point out that in Western and Central Europe "the share of taxes in transport fuel—in particular for gasoline—is generally the highest of all end-use prices. In Europe the tax share in unleaded gasoline [for example] is substantially above the actual production costs, ranging from 50 to 75 percent of the end-user price." They go on to assert that "not surprisingly, in the United States, where gasoline taxes are the lowest in the OECD [Organization for Economic Cooperation and Development], the average fuel consumption ranks among the highest" (1998, 33; also see Dunn 1981 and Lucas 1985). By way of comparison, according to a study of the Energy Information Administration (a U.S. government agency), while the average cost of gasoline was recently $2.26 per gallon in the United States, it was $6.17 in Britain, $5.98 in Germany, $5.94 in Italy, and $5.68 in France. These price differences are mostly, if not solely, attributable to taxation. On a per capita basis, the United States uses more than twice as much gasoline as these other countries (Romero 2005; also see Sheehan 2001).

There is a strategic advantage to limiting oil use in the realm of transportation while allowing it to expand in such areas of the economy as electricity and industrial production. There are readily available substitutes for petroleum products in these latter activities: coal, natural gas, nuclear power, wind power, solar, etc. (Laird 2001; Bradford 2006). This is not the case for automotive transportation. Thus, if there is a severe shortage of crude, the housing stock, industrial infrastructure, and retail outlets that are only accessible via automobile can become virtually worthless overnight.

With the oil shortages of the 1970s the governments of France and West Germany sought to slash their petroleum consumption by greatly expanding the use of nuclear power. This strategy, however, sparked the Green environmental movement on the continent (Nelkin and Pollak 1981), as the question of what to do with the highly radioactive waste from nuclear power production has never been satisfactorily answered (Bupp and Derian 1978; Stoett 2003; Dawson and Darst 2006; Vandenbosch and Vandenbosch 2007; Wald 2008 Feb. 17). This movement was more successful in Germany than in France in derailing plans to center industrial and electricity production on nuclear energy. Political scientist Michael Hatch (1986) contends that these different outcomes can be attributed to each country's political system. The French employ a presidential system, where policymaking power is in large part insulated from the public in the executive branch. The German parliamentary form of government is more sensitive and responsive to social movements and strong shifts in public opinion. Nevertheless, France's shift to nuclear power (Jasper 1990; Hecht 1998; Erlanger 2008); the more modest increase of nuclear power in other countries of the region (Nau 1974); greater use of coal and natural gas; and increases in energy efficiency; did result in a decline in petroleum consumption in Western Europe, whereas oil consumption in the United States increased after the energy shocks of the 1970s (Hatch 1986; Nijkamp 1994; Philip 1994, 195; Convery 1998; Haugland et al. 1998).[5]

## CONCLUSION: OIL DEPLETION

Urban sprawl is predicated on abundant global oil supplies. As many major cities worldwide expand horizontally, petroleum in excess of demand is necessary to maintain gasoline/diesel inexpensive enough to make daily commuting, as well as numerous other automotive trips, economically feasible. As outlined in this chapter, U.S. policies have been historically geared toward placing as much of the world's petroleum reservoirs as possible within the U.S. orbit, thereby ensuring the Western allies economies' access to surplus supplies of oil. These policies have, ostensibly, been shaped by economic elites.

A factor that cannot be addressed diplomatically or militarily is oil depletion. With oil surpluses available, extraction/production can readily rise as demand for gasoline increases, thus keeping the price of petroleum stable and relatively low. Petroleum, however, is a finite resource, and the oil surpluses that have allowed urban sprawl to exist and expand cannot last forever. Given the degree of urban sprawl of U.S. cities in particular and their consequent automotive and oil dependency, the disappearance of surplus oil bodes disaster for the U.S. economy, and by implication the global economy. What will occur with the exhaustion of excess global petroleum is that oil supplies will become tighter as demand stays the same or increases, hence driving up prices to potentially damaging levels. The worst scenario is that global petroleum production will peak and subsequently decline, while the demand for petroleum products remains stable or climbs. This would ultimately create an economically destabilizing gap between supply and demand. Examples of such a gap occurred in the United States in the 1970s, when for short periods of time oil supply fell substantially short of demand, causing the price of gasoline to reach meteoric highs, gas rationing through price controls, and long lines at the pump. In both cases the shortfall of petroleum triggered severe global recessions (Van Til 1982; Vietor 1984; Podobnik 2006, ch. 6).

The type of petroleum production peak that eventually could reek havoc on the U.S. economy is known as Hubbert's Peak, named after M. King Hubbert, a long-time geologist for Shell. Comparing rates of petroleum extraction with the amounts of newly discovered oil, Hubbert in 1956 famously predicted that U.S. crude production would peak in the early 1970s. It did so in 1970, at somewhat less than ten million barrels a day (Deffeyes 2001; Goodstein 2004; Krauss 2007 Nov. 2). Hence, when the U.S. economy was suddenly cut off from Saudi Arabian oil in 1973 and from Iranian supplies in 1979, U.S. production could not exceed (nor meet) the 1970 peak. Today, in spite of significantly increased drilling activity, oil production in the United States is down to 5.1 million barrels a day (Krauss 2007 Nov. 2).[6]

Expert observers have concluded that global peak petroleum production is set to occur in the near future, if it has not already occurred (e.g., Deffeyes 2001, 2005; Goodstein 2004). Energy expert Roy L. Nersesian observed in 2007 that "the frequency of discovering major oil fields is dropping; the size of newly discovered oil fields is falling; and consumption is getting ahead of additions to proven reserves" (206). Following from Hubbert's theory of oil extraction, these observations portend global peak petroleum production. The International Energy Agency (2007 July 9), a public body that advises twenty-six industrialized countries (including the United States) on energy matters, explained in a 2007 report that there are definite signs that global petroleum supplies could fall substantially short of demand within the next five years (Kanter 2007; also see Hoyos and Bias 2008). Petroleum geologist and former colleague of Hubbert (who died in 1989) Kenneth Deffeyes holds that the peak will/has occur(red) between 2003 and 2009 (2001, 158). R. W. Bentley, from Great Britain's Reading University and the Oil Depletion Analysis Center in London, pushes back the point of peak production to between 2010 and 2015 (Rutledge 2005, 139).

There are indications that peak production is occurring sooner rather than later. In July 2008 the cost of a barrel of oil surged to $147, representing a more than sevenfold increase since 2002 (Mouawad and Timmons 2006; Krauss 2008 Oct. 14).[7] (During the oil crisis of the 1970s, the price of a barrel of oil [adjusting for inflation] peaked at just over $100.) Paul Roberts, writing in early 2005, reports that

> [a]t an energy conference in Houston last spring, Saudi oil officials admitted that production at their largest fields was being maintained only by the injection of massive volumes of seawater to force the oil to keep flowing out. They also admitted that Ghawar, the largest oil field ever discovered and a mainstay of the world oil business, was more than half depleted and that the reserves in parts of Ghawar were down to just 40 percent of their original volume.

Roberts adds:

> At the same conference, Matt Simmons, a Houston energy investor and Bush administration energy adviser who has studied trends in world oil production, made the case that Ghawar is actually closer to 90 percent depleted and that the Saudi oil kingdom is much nearer its production peak than anyone in Riyadh—or Washington—wants to believe. (335)

Simmons (2005) in his book about Saudi oil production, entitled *Twilight in the Desert: The Coming Saudi Oil Shock and the World Economy*, makes the specific claim that "Saudi Arabian [petroleum] production is at or very near its *peak sustainable volume* (if it did not, in fact, peak almost 25 years ago), and is likely to go *into decline* in the very foreseeable future" (xv; emphasis in original).

With Saudi oil production waning, and in danger of faltering, it would seem that Iraqi oil production has to attain it pre–first Persian Gulf war level if oil prices are to reliably remain within a reasonable range.[8] Iraqi production dropped significantly because of this 1991 war and the economic sanctions that were placed on this country because of it. Iraq has the second largest known reserves of petroleum. The 2003 U.S. invasion of this country held the potential of reintroducing Iraqi petroleum at full-throttle production to the global oil market. Due to the decrepit state of Iraq's oil infrastructure, and an insurgency that regularly targets Iraqi's oil facilities, petroleum production in Iraq is struggling to attain even pre-invasion rates (Pauly and Lansford 2005; Roberts 2005, 337; Rutledge 2005; "Iraq Oil Output Lowest Since Invasion" 2006; Juhasz 2007; Fletcher and Pagnamenta 2008).

Another approach to countering depleting oil production is to develop alternative fuels. Hydrogen, for instance, could potentially serve as a substitute for gasoline in automobiles. It is noteworthy that the Twentieth Century Fund's task force on "United States Energy Policy" in 1977 *"recommed[ed] an extensive program of government-supported research and development for new energy sources"* (emphasis in original). The task force specifically pointed to oil shale or synthetic gas derived from coal as potential alternatives to petroleum-based gasoline. It also advised government funding "to develop the more exotic alternative energy sources" (1977, 24–25). In response to the oil shocks of the 1970s the federal government did invest significant sums of money in investigating alternative fuels, but as petroleum prices fell by the early 1980s it dramatically cut this spending (Van Til 1982; Podobnik 2006, ch. 7; Krauss 2008 Oct. 21).

Finally, the United States could respond to the ominous signs of declining global oil production by cutting consumption through the reconfiguration of its urban zones to make them less automobile dependent, and more conducive to rapid mass transportation, biking, and walking. I take up the issues of alternative energy and the reconfiguration of U.S. urban areas in the next chapter.

# Chapter Six

## Democratic Ethics, Environmental Groups, and Symbolic Inclusion

### *The Case of Global Warming*

The U.S. government's ostensible goal with regard to the issue of climate change is to ecologically modernize the U.S. system of urban sprawl. At the core of ecological modernization is the idea that environmental protection and economic growth are complementary goals. This complementary relationship can be achieved through the development and application of technology and environmentally safer products. The second Bush administration, for example, advocated the curtailment of the key greenhouse gas—carbon dioxide—through the development of hydrogen-powered automobiles to replace ones that combust gasoline. It also promoted carbon capturing and sequestering technology in the use of coal-fired power plants (Roberts 2004; Bumiller and Hulse 2005; Samuelsohn 2006; Moroney 2008; Mufson 2008).[1] Another feature of the Bush administration's approach to abating climate-changing emissions was the expanded use of nuclear power and biofuels (Wald 2005; Andrews and Barringer 2007; Andrews and Rohter 2007). An energy bill passed in 2005 by the U.S. Senate promoted wind, solar power, and biofuel as sources of energy—all of which could greatly reduce carbon dioxide emissions if used to replace fossil fuels (Everly 2005; Hulse 2005).[2] The federal government enacted an energy law in 2007 that encourages the production of ethanol—a biofuel (Broder 2007; Krauss 2007 Dec. 18).

The ecological modernizing of consumer products leads to economic growth and increases competitiveness because consumers are increasingly demanding environmentally benign products. For instance, hybrid automobiles, which use both electricity and gasoline for power, are in high demand in the United States (Hakim 2005 August 4; Maynard 2007; Hasegawa 2008). Moreover, ecologically modernizing society in and of itself will create new employment opportunities as environmentally damaging energy and production infrastructures are replaced with environmentally benign ones (Weale 1992; Hajer 1995; Dryzek 1996a, 480; 2005, ch. 8; Mol 2001, 2002; York and Rosa 2003; Hatch 2005; Barringer 2008 Oct. 20).

Ecological modernization is consistent with free market environmentalism, which holds that environmental protection is consistent with the utilization of the market (Chichilnisky and Heal 2000; Anderson and Leal 2001; Dryzek 2005, ch. 6). In addition to supporting government programs that research the development of alternative fuels and carbon sequestering technologies, President Bush's 2002 Clear Skies Initiative program relied on companies/consumers to use fossil fuels more efficiently to reduce their costs. This in itself will result in an average 18 percent reduction of carbon dioxide emissions by 2012 for every unit of energy produced in the U.S. economy (Roberts 2004, 137–38; Revkin 2005).

State and local governments in the United States are also seeking to ecologically modernize their economies (Barringer 2008 Feb. 7) to reduce climate-changing emissions as well as other airborne emissions. Barry Rabe's (2004, 2008) description of state and local responses to global warming demonstrates this (also see Keeler 2007). Certain regions of the country have been overt in putting forward policies to abate climate-changing emissions—in particular the far West and the Northeast. Elsewhere in the country, states and localities have pursued policies that, while not necessarily intended to abate greenhouse gases, have nonetheless done so. In both explicit and "stealthy" states, policies have almost exclusively relied on technology to abate both localized air pollution and climate-changing gases—either with efficiency initiatives or through the use of alternative fuels (mostly wind power and solar energy) (also see Lyons, Peterson, and Noerager 2003; Williams 2008).[3]

In an earlier book on localized air pollution, I (2005a) demonstrated that a technological approach to pollution reduction has been advocated by business elites in the United States since the late nineteenth century. At the forefront of air pollution abatement efforts have been economic elites who derive wealth from the development and sale of land. As outlined in chapter 3 of this book, these elites are at the center of what Harvey Molotch refers to as local growth coalitions—economic interests who attain income from economic growth and activities in specific localities. Large amounts of localized air pollution are an economic negative for these interests since they deter investment and tourism from any specific locality. (The prime anthropogenic climate-changing gas, carbon dioxide, is invisible and odorless. Airborne pollutants such as carbon monoxide, sulfur dioxide, and nitrogen oxide, in contrast, can—when emitted in large enough amounts—pose local health hazards and aesthetic blights.)

In my 2005 volume I went on to argue that those environmental groups that lobby government, at all levels, to bring about cleaner air should end their lobbying efforts. This is because environmental groups have been incorporated into the government's policymaking process on the basis of an agenda developed by economic elites—the promotion of the development and deployment of technology to effectuate airborne pollution abatement. The most tangible result of these groups' incorporation is to legitimize the policymaking process by making this process appear inclusive and democratic (Edelman 1977; Saward 1992), whereas it is unclear whether their participation in the policymaking process (e.g., lobbying policymakers) results in environmental protection.

On the issue of climate change, outlined in the next section, environmental groups that lobby government ostensibly limit their advocacy to the development and deployment of technology to abate greenhouse gases. Therefore, they seemingly elide the issue of urban sprawl in seeking to influence and shape U.S. climate change policies. The inherent environmental difficulties in relying on technology to abate anthropogenic greenhouse gases (as opposed to reducing urban sprawl) are described below.

International business organizations—the World Business Council for Sustainable Development and the International Chamber of Commerce—also advocate for the development and deployment of technology to abate climate-changing emissions. These technologies would ideally reduce/eliminate greenhouse gas emissions and allow urban sprawl to persist.

The final section of this chapter treats alternative strategies that environmental groups which lobby government could/should pursue in order to abate climate-changing emissions. These strategies involve placing their political focus on arenas outside of government, and instead mobilizing broader segments of the public to achieve environmental protection.

# ECOLOGICAL MODERNIZATION, URBAN SPRAWL, AND SYMBOLIC INCLUSION

In his analysis of interest group inclusion within the policymaking process, democratic theorist John Dryzek explains that "oppositional groupings can only be included in the state in benign fashion when the defining interest of the group can be related quite directly to a state imperative" (1996a, 479). In other words, according to Dryzek, groups that critique the status quo can only participate in the policymaking process to the extent that the groups' goals are consistent with an objective of the state. This is reflected in the behavior of the environmental groups that are active in the formulation of the federal government's climate change regime.

Environmental activists involved in this formulation process are aware of the relationship between a greater number/use of automobiles (with internal combustion engines) (indicative of urban sprawl), and climate change gases. On its Web site the Sierra Club asserts that "if U.S. autos were a separate country, they would be the world's fifth largest global warmer polluter, emitting more than all sources in Great Britain combined."[4] The Natural Resources Defense Council (NRDC) notes that "automobiles create nearly 1.5 billion tons of $CO_2$ annually" in the United States.[5]

The predominate answers put forward by major environmental groups that lobby Washington, D.C., on the question of climate change are technology and alternative fuels.[6] The Sierra Club, for instance, holds on its Web site, in a page entitled "Global Warming & Energy: Overview: Solutions," that "energy efficiency is the cleanest, safest, most economical way to begin to curb global warming." It adds that "while there is not technology to remove $CO_2$ from a car's exhaust, we can make them pollute less by making them more fuel efficient." Therefore, "If we are to make any progress in slowing global warming, we must make our cars go farther on a gallon of gas." Additionally, "Harnessing the clean, abundant energy of the sun and wind is critical to solving the global warming problem."[7]

The Union of Concerned Scientists (UCS) has a Web page detailing its position on climate change, entitled "Global Warming Solutions." In terms of direct action to abate greenhouse gases, on this Web page the UCS holds that "by putting energy efficiency, renewable energy, and vehicle technology solutions in place at the federal level, we can reduce our contribution to global warming."[8] A Washington, D.C.–based lobbyist for the UCS acknowledged in a telephone interview that the UCS limits its lobbying activity on climate change to pressing for more fuel-efficient vehicles and alternative energy (Anderson 2005).[9]

U.S. PIRG has a Web page entitled "Stopping Global Warming Pollution." On this page, under the heading "Solutions Are Available Now," U.S. PIRG argues that "[t]he good news is we can reduce global warming pollution by using existing technology to make power plants and factories more efficient, make cars go farther on a gallon of gasoline, and shift to cleaner technologies, such as hybrids, biofuels, and wind and solar power."[10]

The NRDC Web site, in a modification made sometime since March 2007, does give some prominence to discussing the reform of U.S. urban zones to abate greenhouse gas emissions. In a web page titled "Solving Global Warming," there is a section labeled "Better

Cars & Smart Growth." Its author(s) in the first two paragraphs of this three-paragraph section advocate for more efficient automobiles, as well as for alternative fuels, to abate climate-changing emissions and reduce gasoline consumption:

> Our gasoline-burning cars are the second-largest source of U.S. global warming pollution. But Americans will put more than 300 million new cars on the road over the next 20 years—if these cars are the best, most efficient vehicles Detroit can make, we'll take a big step toward solving global warming.
>
> Using hybrid engines and other ready-to-go technologies in today's cars could nearly double the mileage they'd get from a gallon of gas, saving a lot of money at the pump. By 2050, fuel-cell technologies and other advancements could boost efficiency to 54 miles per gallon.

In the last paragraph of this section its author(s) explain: "We can curb our appetite for oil even further by adopting 'smart growth' principles in our cities and towns, encouraging developers to build compact, walkable communities that allow people to spend less time behind the wheel."[11]

The Web page "Solving Global Warming" has three more sections, other than the "Better Cars & Smart Growth" section. These sections are "Boost Energy Efficiency," "Biofuels and Renewable Energy," and "Return Carbon to the Ground" (i.e., carbon sequestration). In all of these sections alternative energy and technological solutions are put forward as the answer to climate change.

Suggestive of NRDC's muted commitment to placing urban sprawl on the political agenda, on another NDRC Web site page treating solutions to climate change—entitled "Global Warming Basics: What it is, How it's Caused, and What Needs to be Done to Stop it"—no mention is made of reforming urban sprawl, nor of so-called smart growth. On the NDRC's Global Warming Basics Web page is the following rhetorical question: "How can we cut global warming pollution?" In response to this self-posed question, the NRDC responds:

> It's simple: By reducing pollution from vehicles and power plants. Right away, we should put existing technologies for building cleaner cars and more modern electricity generators into widespread use. We can increase our reliance on renewable energy sources such as wind, sun and geothermal. And we can manufacture more efficient appliances and conserve energy.[12]

I highlight four environmental groups (Natural Resources Defense Council, the Sierra Club, Union of Concerned Scientists, and U.S. PIRG) and their political advocacy as it relates to climate change because in informal telephone conversations with Washington-based environmental organizations these four were noted as the most active and visible in Washington, D.C., on the issue of global warming and energy. All four have lobbying offices in D.C.[13]

Almost every major U.S. environmental group in 2002, however, went on record as focusing politically on technology and alternative energy to address climate change emissions in the United States. As part of the environmental conference entitled "The Johannesburg Summit 2002: A Call for Action," an open letter was issued urging the Bush Administration to undertake aggressive action to protect the environment. With regard to taking direct steps to abate climate change emissions, the authors of this open letter urged the U.S. government to "stimulate development and deployment of energy efficiency and renewable energy technologies." Omitted from this open letter is any discussion of urban sprawl in the United States and the huge energy demand it creates. Among the signatories to it were virtually all of the leading national environmental groups in the United States: National Environmental Trust, Natural Resources Defense Council, Friends of the Earth, the World Wildlife Fund, the Nature Conservancy, Greenpeace USA, the Sierra Club, and Environmental Defense (Redefining Progress 2002).

By promoting/emphasizing technology and alternative energy as the means to reduce greenhouse gases, these environmental groups and activists are simply advocating for the ecological modernization of U.S. sprawled urban zones, which is wholly consist with the state imperative/goal described above. At best, they can be viewed as the most aggressive advocates within the policymaking process of the ecological modernization of urban sprawl. This is congruous with Dryzek's observation that when the state has imperatives oppositional groups within the policymaking process are limited to "influencing how imperatives are met, and how trade-offs between competing imperatives are made" (1996a, 480).

Therefore, in order to be effective within the policy formulation process, environmentalists, within this specific context, drop/minimize critiques of urban sprawl and the increased usage of the automobile. As explained by Dryzek, under a political process where the state has imperatives, "a high price will be paid by any [oppositional] group included [within the state] on this basis. For if state officials have no compelling reason to include the group, then presumably it must moderate its stance to fit with established state imperatives" (1996a, 480).

# BUSINESS' RESPONSE TO CLIMATE CHANGE

## THE GCC

Historically, three international business policy-planning organizations have directly taken up the question of climate change: the Global Climate Coalition (GCC), the World Business Council for Sustainable Development (WBCSD), and the International Chamber of Commerce (ICC) (Levy and Egan 2003). According to its Web site, the GCC was an "organization of trade associations established in 1989 to coordinate business participation in the international policy debate on the issue of global climate change and global warming." Operating between 1998 and 2002, it claimed to "represent more than 6 million businesses, companies and corporations in virtually every sector of U.S. business, agriculture and forestry, including electric utilities, railroads, transportation, manufacturing, small businesses, mining, oil, and coal." Finally, "the GCC represent[ed] the views of its members to legislative bodies and policymakers. And it review[ed] and provide[d] comments on proposed legislation and government programs."[14] Levy and Egan (2003), who have studied the international business community's response to the issue of climate change, note that although the GCC "was constituted as a U.S.–based organization and was focused on domestic lobbying, a number of U.S. subsidiaries of European multinationals also joined, and the GCC quickly rose to be the most prominent voice of industry" (815) ("Anti-Kyoto Industry Group Folds" 2002).

The GCC had been an active opponent of government regulatory action to bring about reductions in greenhouse gas emissions. Along with a number of conservative think tanks (McCright and Dunlap 2000), its approach toward resisting such action had been to question the science surrounding climate change (Levy and Egan 2003, 815). The GCC stated on its Web site that the "businesses and industries that make up the GCC's member trade associations are active participants in voluntary programs for reducing greenhouse gas emissions that are part of the federal government's U.S. Climate Action Plan."[15]

## THE WBCSD

Unlike the GCC, the ICC and WBCSD have not positioned themselves as opponents of climate change science or governmental efforts to address greenhouse gas emissions. Instead, these organizations have more clearly established themselves as business-led policy discussion groups on the question of climate change.

The WBCSD is made up of a number of global corporations, headquartered all over the world. In 1996 the WBCSD had about 125 corporate members drawn from eight regions of the globe: Western Europe, Central/Eastern Europe, Africa/Middle East, North America, Latin America, Japan, Asia, and Oceania. Among its members are Renault, Total, Volkswagen, Fiat, Statoil (Norway/Petroleum), Volvo, British Petroleum, Shell Oil, Texaco, Mitsubishi, and Toyota (Schmidheiny et al. 1996, xvi–xx). According to its Web site, the WBCSD is currently a "coalition" of two hundred "international companies." Its "members are drawn from more than 35 countries and 20 major industrial sectors." The WBCSD also "benefits from a global network of about 55 national and regional business councils and regional partners."[16]

The WBCSD posits itself as a proponent of the ecological modernization of global capitalism; its mission statement casts its primary purpose in terms consistent with ecological modernization theory. Thus, the council's mission is "to provide business leadership as a catalyst for change toward sustainable development, and to support the business license to operate, innovate and grow in a world increasingly shaped by sustainable development issues."[17] An earlier version of the WBCSD's mission statement asserted that the council's mission was "to provide business leadership as a catalyst for change toward sustainable development, and to promote the role of eco-efficiency, innovation, and corporate social responsibility."[18]

The WBCSD, however, advocates a narrow or "weak" conception of ecological modernization to address global warming. A narrow approach to ecological modernization relies heavily on technological solutions and alternative fuels to address environmental degradation (Christoff 1996; Dryzek et al. 2003; Dryzek 2005, ch. 8). In a 2003 WBCSD document entitled *Energy and Climate: The WBCSD's Itinerary*, its author(s) outline the steps necessary to address global warming as follows: "in the short term, focus on energy efficiency; in the medium term, sequestration of greenhouse gases as a path to a sustainable energy future; and begin work on the long term energy solutions, cleaner fuels and alternative energy sources" (2003, 3). In a more recent document (2007), entitled *Policy Directions to 2050: Energy & Climate*, the WBCSD asserts that

> reducing the energy intensity of the global economy and the GHG [greenhouse gas] intensity of energy will require major breakthroughs in energy efficiency, renewables, next generation nuclear, clean coal, carbon capture and storage (CCS) and mobility. Such breakthroughs must be *developed* and then *deployed*. (2; emphasis in original)

A more expansive, or "stronger," conception of ecological modernization would involve ecologically sensitive land management. This type of land management would entail the intensive usage of land (as opposed to sprawl), drawing residential and work areas closer together, and creating smaller work and living spaces in urban areas. Ecologically sensitive land management would move residents away from their dependence on the automobile (and the internal combustion engine) and toward more ecologically benign forms of transportation, such as walking, bicycling, and mass transit (Newman and Kenworthy 1999; Bulkeley and Betsill 2003).

The WBCSD conducts what it refers to as sector projects (WBCSD Sector Projects). It has six in total. Here, certain WBCSD members, along with certain experts, discuss and treat topics that, presumably, are central to sustainable development. These six sector projects are entitled (1) forest products industry, (2) mining, metals, and minerals, (3) cement sustainability initiative, (4) sustainable mobility, (5) electric utilities, and (6) financial sector. The sustainable mobility and electric utilities sector projects are the most germane to the question of climate change. The sustainable mobility project is made up of British Petroleum, DaimlerChrysler, Ford, General Motors, Honda, Michelin Tire Company, Nissan Motor, Norsk Hydro, Renault, Shell, Toyota, and Volkswagen. Among this project's self-defined "challenges" in attaining sustainable mobility is "reducing carbon emissions." In responding to this challenge this sector project posits: "Vehicle Design and Technology: determine how developments in road vehicle technology and design can affect sustainability." Another answer is: "Fuels: explore the options for making fuels both sustainable and affordable" (2002, 12–13).[19] In the realm of electric utilities, the key solution to the problem of attaining sustainable development is "continuing to invest in research into new technologies that will help to move the sector significantly further down the sustainable development path" (2002, 15).

Hence, to prevent climate change the objective of the WBCSD is not to necessarily reduce energy consumption in the broad operation of the global economy, but to minimize the greenhouse gases emanated in the production and use of energy. (The former tactic is indicative of strong ecological modernization.) The shortcomings in WBCSD's approach to global warming are twofold. First, technological solutions could simply serve to shift the ecological stress created by one activity from one aspect of the ecosystem on to another (Dryzek 1987). The case of nuclear power demonstrates this point. While greater reliance on nuclear power will reduce greenhouse gas emissions (Wald 2008 Oct. 24), the production of nuclear power and the disposal of nuclear wastes both have significant environmental liabilities, which in the long term could be just as environmentally degrading as climate change (Bupp and Derian 1978; Russell

1989; Stoett 2003; Vaitheeswarn 2003, ch. 10; Gertner 2006; Palfreman 2006; Vandenbosch and Vandenbosch 2007). Hydrogen, which is widely discussed as a possible energy alternative to fossil fuels (Monastersky 2003; Wald 2003; WBCSD 2005, 8–9), could have similar liabilities. Another potentially environmentally hazardous substitute for fossil fuels is ethanol, a liquid fuel that can be used to power automobiles, trucks, and buses. One environmental liability of ethanol fuels is that more and more wilderness—especially in tropical rainforests—must be cleared to grow large amounts of source crops (e.g., sugar, soybeans, corn) to meet ethanol demand (Barrett 2007; Leahy 2007).[20]

The second difficulty associated with any technological approach to abating greenhouse gases, including an approach rooted in alternative fuels, is that no technology has come forth that effectively confronts the question of climate change within the current context of global capitalism.[21] In other words, no technology to date has been developed to allow current rates of economic growth and consumption to continue without the externality of climate change (or, alternatively, the creation of intractable amounts of nuclear waste). For example, as I have already noted, hydrogen has been posited as a potentially clean, unlimited, and affordable replacement for fossil fuels. A scientist of the Natural Resources Defense Council, however, opined about hydrogen fuel use that "real revolutions have to occur before this is going to become a large-scale reality." He went on to note, "It very possibly could happen, but" a hydrogen-based economy is "not a sure thing" (quoted in Wald 2003). Writing in the journal *Nature,* Brian C. H. Steele, of the University of London's Imperial College, and Angelika Heinzel, of the University of Duisburg-Essen, in Germany, concluded that "unless there is a breakthrough in the production of hydrogen and the development of new hydrogen-storage materials, the concept of a 'hydrogen economy' will remain an unlikely scenario" (2001, 345; also see Romm 2004). While we wait for such breakthroughs, the environmental effects of climate change emissions could irreversibly come to a head.

## THE ICC'S COMMISSION ON ENVIRONMENT AND ENERGY

In contrast to the WBCSD, the ICC has a broad membership base. According to its Web site, "ICC membership groups thousands of companies of every size in over 130 countries worldwide. They represent a broad cross-section of business activity including manufacturing, trade, services and the professions." The ICC's Web site goes on to explain that its member

> companies shape rules and policies that stimulate international trade and investment. These companies in turn count on the

prestige and expertise of ICC to get business views across to governments and intergovernmental organizations, whose decisions affect corporate finances and operations worldwide.[22]

Among ICC members are AT&T, British Gas, Chevron, Citicorp, DuPont, ExxonMobil, Fiat, Ford, General Electric, General Motors, the Japan Chamber of Commerce and Industry, Nissan Motor, Norsk Hydro, Procter & Gamble, Sony, and Toyota.[23]

The ICC conducts much of its policy work through commissions. Its Web site notes that its "commissions are the bedrock of ICC." They are "composed of a total of more than 500 business experts who give freely of their time to formulate ICC policy and elaborate its rules." One of the ICC's sixteen commissions is the Commission on Environment and Energy. The author(s) of this Web site go on to explain that "commissions scrutinize proposed international and national government initiatives affecting their subject areas and prepare business positions for submission to international organizations and governments."[24] The vice-chair of the ICC Commission on Environment and Energy is Brian Flannery, an executive of oil giant ExxonMobil.[25]

Like the WBCSD, the ICC Commission on Environment and Energy advocates the development and deployment of technology (including alternative fuels) to cope with the phenomenon of climate change. In an ICC December 12, 2003, press release, entitled "Business Backs Technology Solutions for Climate Change," Nick Campbell, chairperson of the commission's Committee on Climate Change is quoted as arguing that "it is evident today that the widespread use of existing, efficient technology is indispensable, and that a wide range of technologies will be needed" to deal with climate change. The press release also approvingly reports that "business has for years been insisting that innovative technologies provide the most effective economic solution to long-term risk to the climate through global warming." In December 2007 the ICC's Commission on Environment and Energy released a document titled "Business Perspectives on a Long-Term International Framework to Address Global Climate Change." The authors of this document hold that

much more can be done to reduce [climate change] emissions through more widespread use of existing technology, but advances will be essential to meet growing energy demand and respond to climate risks. In meeting these challenges business, including ICC members, will play a leading role in the global deployment of the existing efficient technologies and practices, and in research, development and widespread dissemination of advanced technologies that must be created in coming decades. (5)

The ICC Environmental and Energy Commission's Energy Committee published a report in 2002 entitled *Energy for Sustainable Development*. In its report the committee posits technology as the only solution to the economic and environmental issues related to energy usage. The committee begins its report by noting the importance of inexpensive energy to the global operation of the economy:

> In economic terms, energy can represent a fairly small part of a nation's GDP, normally less than 5 percent. It is therefore an often underrated element of national politics and economics. However it must be emphasized that although energy can to some degree be substituted with capital and labor, it is by and large an irreplaceable and vital element of a nation's economy, with links to virtually every other aspect. Therefore, active involvement in energy policy discussions, research and planning is in the long term interest of Business and Industry, as well as of society at large. (ICC 2002, 1)

In terms of achieving environmental and energy sustainability,[26] the Energy Committee eschews conservation and instead holds:

> In the coming decades there are several emerging technologies likely to exert a major impact on the energy supply scene. Among these are: clean coal (combined with carbon dioxide sequestering technologies) and advanced and new nuclear reactors with further improved safety features for public acceptance and better economy, synthetic gasoline and diesel oil as well as carbon free alternatives for fueling the transport sector. New renewables, although not likely to provide a significant contribution to energy supply for many decades to come, are nevertheless of great interest for the future and therefore worthy of support for research and development. (ICC 2002, 2)

With regard to the specific issue of climate change, the author(s) of the committee's report write:

> Achieving greenhouse gas (GHG) reductions could be costly and with impacts on competitiveness, employment, trade and investment. For these reasons, the most economically feasible way to meet the long-term challenge of climate change is through the development and global deployment of innovative technologies that reduce or avoid such emissions. (ICC 2002, 6)

The author(s) of the report go on to render the observation that the

ICC believes that the most economically feasible way to address the long-term challenge of sustainable development is through the development, commercialization and wide-spread dissemination of both efficient existing technologies and new, currently non-commercial technologies that can deliver modern energy solutions, improve efficiency and reduce emissions. (ICC 2002, 7)

# REBELLIOUS POLITICS, THE ENVIRONMENTAL LOBBY, AND DEMOCRACY

In my 2005 book on localized air pollution I argue that environmental groups should withdraw from the policymaking process. This is because this process is undemocratic. It is being driven by local growth coalitions, the automobile industry (Luger 2000), and the energy sector (Olien and Olien 2000). It is because of the dominant role of these economic interests that the government approach to abating air pollution is centered on technology. Thus, certain actors or forces block central political and economic issues from making it onto the agenda (Bachrach and Baratz 1962; Crenson 1971; Lindblom 1982; Hayward 2000; Lukes 2005; Wolbrecht and Hero 2005). Instead of expending energy and resources lobbying government, environmental groups should focus their efforts on educating the public about the perils of urban sprawl, and they should refuse to participate in any political process that excludes key issues/questions, such as urban sprawl.

This is consistent with Mark Dowie's (1995) position that environmental groups should pull back from Washington, D.C., politics and concentrate on mobilizing the grass roots and increasing the pro-environment coalition by drawing alliances with other progressive groups. Michael Shellenberger and Ted Nordhaus (2004) in their well-publicized pamphlet (Barringer 2005; Garofoli 2005; Nordhaus and Shellenberger 2007) critical of the Washington environmental lobbying community, entitled *The Death of Environmentalism*, offer thinking that is similar to that Dowie's and my own:

> The environmental movement's incuriosity about the interests of potential allies depends on it never challenging the most basic assumptions about what does and doesn't get counted as "environmental." Because we define environmental problems so narrowly, environmental leaders come up with equally narrow solutions. In the face perhaps of the greatest calamity in modern history [global warming], environmental leaders are sanguine that selling technical solutions like florescent light bulbs, more efficient appliances,

and hybrid cars will be sufficient to muster the necessary political strength to overcome the alliance of neoconservative ideologues and industry interests in Washington, D.C. (10)

Julian Agyeman (2005) argues that a broad-based environmental movement would embrace the Just Sustainability Paradigm that incorporates resource conservation, environmental protection, and social justice (also see Agyeman, Bullard, and Evans 2003). He asserts that the most efficacious means of addressing these objectives simultaneously would be by reforming cities. Raquel Pinderhughes (2004) describes multiple ways in which cities could be reconfigured to improve people's lives, reduce pollution, and lessen resource consumption (also see Pieterse 2008).

Reducing urban sprawl is perhaps the most obvious way to achieve conservation, abate airborne emissions, and make cities more livable. The authors of the edited volume *Just Transportation* (Bullard and Johnson 1997) describe how automobile dependency, traffic congestion, and long driving distances create personal and financial hardships for middle- and lower-class residents of U.S. urban zones (also see Duany, Plater-Zyberk, and Speck 2000; Frumkin, Frank, and Jackson 2004; Burchell et al. 2005; Vallianatos et al. 2005; Sloman 2006; Soule 2006). The authors of *Sprawl City: Race, Politics, and Planning in Atlanta* (Bullard, Johnson, and Torres 2000) show how urban sprawl has historically been used in that city to maintain de facto racial and class segregation, with poor and minority areas suffering from "urban disinvestment, depressed property values, stagnate business opportunities, and environmental problems" (x; also see Gotham 2000, 2002).

Mainstream environmental groups could withdraw from the state's policymaking process and help in the development of a broader social movement in civil society that would challenge and debate the imperative of urban sprawl. Jeffrey Isaac defines civil society as "those human networks that exist independently of . . . the political state" (1993, 356; also see Isaac 2003). Dryzek argues that civil society is a more democratic venue than the state, because it "is relatively unconstrained." He goes on to explain that within civil society

> discourse need not be suppressed in the interests of strategic advantage [as is the case within the state]; goals and interests need not be compromised or subordinated to the pursuit of office or access; embarrassing troublemakers need not be repressed; the indeterminacy of outcome inherent in democracy need not be subordinated to state policy. (1996a, 486; also see Dryzek 2006)

Thus, democracy here is defined as the ability to consider and advance an indeterminate number of policy means and goals. Hence, Dryzek holds that this openness can only take place outside of the state, because the state is tied to specific objectives.

To the extent that some of the possibilities considered and advanced within civil society contest and confront the state's imperatives, Isaac avers that within civil society "rebellious" politics can take place. He holds that:

> [a] rebellious politics is a politics of voluntary associations, independent of the state, that seeks to create spaces of opposition to remote, disempowering bureaucratic and corporate structures. Such a politics is often directed against the state, but it does not seek to control the state in the way that political parties do. Neither does it lobby the state to achieve specific advantages, as do interest groups. Rather, it is a politics of moral suasion, seeking . . . to affect the political world through the force of its example and through its very specific, proximate results. (1993, 357; also see Kohn 2003)

When they achieve critical mass, rebellious politics are transformed into broad-based social movements. Sidney Tarrow explains that social "movements mount challenges through disruptive direct action against elites, authorities, other groups or cultural codes" (1994, 4).

Within U.S. civil society, and disconnected from the state, there exists a rebellious politics that advocates for more humane communities. In cities throughout the United States there are networks of activists and organizations that advocate for more livable and healthy urban zones with cleaner air, less pollution, and affordable housing and transportation (Bullard 1990, 2005, 2007; Szasz 1994; Schlosberg 1999; Tesh 2000; Frumkin, Frank, and Jackson 2004; Agyeman 2005; Bruegmann 2005; Flint 2006). Writing in 1997, Robert D. Bullard, a professor of sociology and the director of the Environmental Justice Resource Center at Clark Atlanta University, reported:

> Grassroots community groups all over the country are now banding together to address urban problems that are worsened by sprawl. Many of these grassroots groups work on a variety of sprawl issues. Some define themselves as environmentalists, others do not. This emerging new leadership base is defining urban transportation, air quality, health, economic investments, and sprawl-related concerns as core environmental justice and civil rights issues. They are not just talking, they are also taking action. (x)

These politics have been documented in detail in the cases of Los Angeles (Vallianatos et al. 2005), Boston (Agyeman 2005), Atlanta (Bullard and Johnson 2000), Tucson, and Albuquerque (Logan 1995).

For environmental groups concerned about global warming, focusing on cities and metropolitan regions to roll back urban sprawl, and therefore reduce climate-changing gases, appears as a logical strategy in the U.S. context because city and county governmental units in the United States are directly responsible for land use decisions (Logan and Molotch 1987; Warner and Molotch 2000; Press 2002; DeGrove 2005; Wilbanks 2006; Barringer 2008 Aug. 29). Local governments also set building codes and influence transportation infrastructures, both of which impact energy usage and climate-changing emissions (Bulkeley and Betsill 2003; Portney 2003; Shatzkin 2004; Soule 2006; Goodman 2008 June 25). Environmental groups with national and international perspectives can help ensure that urban reforms instituted to reduce urban sprawl and abate greenhouse gas emissions (often referred to as "smart growth" strategies [Shatzkin 2004; DeGrove 2005; Levine 2006; Ruth 2006]) are instituted in a uniform manner across the United States and beyond (Keck and Sikkink 1998; Guadalupe and Rodrigues 2004; Roberts 2007; Roberts and Parks 2007).

Dryzek asserts that "whether a group should choose the state, civil society, or both simultaneously depends on the particular configuration of movement interests and state imperatives" (1996a, 485). He goes on to aver that the most efficacious approach for the environmental community to take is a "dualistic" approach (Cohen and Arato 1992; Wainwright 1994), where part of the community operates within the state to advance the ecological modernization of capitalist society. The more confrontational portion of this community should then operate largely within civil society where they can confront the imperative of urban sprawl, and its attending environmental ill effects. Moreover, the activities of the more contentious portions of the environmental community, by bringing outside pressure to bear, can help that portion within the state to advance the goal of ecological modernization (Dryzek 1996a, 483–86). The difficulty with this dualistic approach is that it fails to take into account how incorporation within the state can serve as a means to undermine rebellious politics and social movements in civil society.

## THE CONTAINMENT OF REBELLIOUS POLITICS

Historically, the state has not been passive in the face of rebellious politics and the emergence of social movements. Instead, it has attempted to ensure that rebellious politics do not achieve critical mass, which could destabilize society or force the state to substantially alter its imperatives as a concession to confrontational social movements (Tarrow 1994). One means to contain rebellious politics is through coercion (Sexton 1991; Acher 2001, 2008).

Another means is to "buy off" those groups and individuals that could potentially be part of a rebellious politics. Progressives, socialists, and Marxists have historically viewed mainstream labor unions and welfare programs as overt attempts on the part of the state and corporations to blunt class conflict and politically subdue and pacify the working class to maintain internal order (Weinstein 1968; Piven and Cloward 1971; Domhoff 2005). Maintaining internal order is a key imperative of the state (Skocpol 1979).

Certain critical thinkers argue that the state manages the public's environmental concerns primarily through the dissemination of symbols (Edelman 1964; O'Connor 1994; Cahn 1995). Cahn (1995), specifically, avers that the federal government's post-1970 environmental regulatory policies (i.e., clean air, clean water, energy, and waste policies) can be most aptly characterized as symbolic responses to the public's growing environmental concerns, rather than as substantive efforts to regulate corporate America. He arrives at this conclusion by analyzing the content of these policies. Furthermore, Cahn juxtaposes the content of these policies with the federal government's continued encouragement of economic growth, and its continued support and subsidization of fossil fuels usage (e.g., road and highway maintenance and expansion). These are the primary factors that cause air and water pollution, as well as create waste. Thus, critics such as Cahn argue that federal environmental legislation and environmental policies designed to regulate corporate America are symbolic precisely because they do not challenge the state's imperative of economic growth, nor have they sought to alter policymakers' reliance on urban sprawl to attain growth.

The federal government's seeming commitment to alternative fuels and carbon sequestration technology can also be interpreted as a symbolic response to the public's environmental concerns (Edelman 1988; Pope and Rauber 2004; "Energy Rhetoric, and Reality" 2007; "A Faith-Based Fuel Initiative" 2007; Krauss 2007 Jan. 22; Revkin 2007; "Posturing and Abdication" 2008). There is precedence for this in U.S. environmental politics. The California Air Resources Board (CARB), for example, promulgated a plan in 1990 that mandated that 2 percent of automobiles offered for sale in 1998 be Zero Emission Vehicles (ZEVs), 5 percent by 2001, and 10 percent by 2003 (Kamieniecki and Farrell 1991; Grant 1996). Currently, only electrically powered vehicles have zero emissions. Similarly, California in 1989 adopted the Air Quality Management Plan (AQMP) (Kraft 1993). The state's AQMP also relied heavily on the long-term development of technology to achieve improvements in air quality. Significantly, neither of these plans put forward subsidies to facilitate the development of hoped-for technologies, nor did they mandate sanctions for industrial sectors that failed to develop the necessary technologies. Commenting on the state's AQMP shortly after it was promulgated, Sheldon Kamieniecki and Michael Farrell astutely observed that "for mainly political reasons, the more difficult decisions [of the AQMP] have been postponed for a number of years, with the hope that new technologies will allow policymakers to meet federal clean-air standards with minimum disruption to . . . economic growth" (1991, 154). Notably, the targets for the manufacture and sale of ZEVs have been postponed and reduced significantly by CARB (Hakim 2003 April 25).[27] On the issue of climate change, a 2002 California law mandating a reduction in greenhouse gas from automobiles was not scheduled to go into effect until 2009, with its strongest abatement rules delayed until 2016 (Cushman 2002); nonetheless, the federal government blocked/annulled this California law in 2007 (Barringer 2007 Dec. 21). Another California law, enacted in 2006, mandates a 25 percent reduction in the state's carbon dioxide emissions to be achieved by 2020 (Barringer 2006 Sept. 15). In 2005, eight Northeastern states (New York, New Jersey, Delaware, Maine, New Hampshire, Vermont, Maryland, and Pennsylvania) announced a plan to abate carbon dioxide emissions from power plants by 10 percent in 2019 (DePalma 2005).

The group mobilization incentive structure outlined by Olson (1971) offers a partial explanation as to why, even with the continuing emission at dangerous levels of greenhouse gases, the U.S. public's environmental concerns have not been transformed into a social movement (Guber 2003). The mere promise of carbon-free fuels and carbon-reducing technologies contributes to the public's relative political passivity on the issue of climate change[28] by communicating symbolically that something is already being done to address the issue of climate change, so that citizens need not spend their time and energy attempting to overcome the collective action barriers inherent in the mobilization of large groups.

To the symbols emanated by policymakers' advertised commitment to environmental friendly fuels and technologies, and regulatory guidelines that push difficult decisions into the future (such as a federal government plan enacted in 2007 to increase the average fuel efficiency of automobiles and light trucks [including SUVs and minivans] to thirty-five miles per gallon in 2020 [Broder 2007]),[29] can be added the inclusion of environmental groups within the policymaking process. In other words, to the extent that environmental activists are included, this inclusion becomes one of the symbols deployed against the public, and works to keep it from mobilizing on the issue of climate change. The participation of environmental activists in the policymaking process, which consists of both formal and informal access to the Environmental Protection Agency, the U.S. Congress, and state governments (Duffy 2003; Rabe 2004; Bosso 2005), communicates to the broader public that this process is democratic because it is, putatively, inclusive of all relevant political perspectives (Edelman 1977; Wynne 1982; Saward 1992).[30] In fact, the public policy-making process is not democratic, because the key issues of urban sprawl and automobile dependence are kept off the agenda (Gonzalez 2005a).

## THE ENVIRONMENTAL LOBBY AND THE ECOLOGICAL MODERNIZATION OF URBAN SPRAWL

Why would environmental activists want to lend legitimacy through their participation to an undemocratic policy formulation process? A more intuitive question might be, Why would environmental activists want to participate in a process that keeps central issues from being effectively discussed?

Dowie (1995), in his critique of large "mainstream" U.S. environmental groups, alleges that these groups have been knowingly incorporated on a symbolic basis. He specifically holds that the leaders of the major environmental groups prioritize organizational maintenance over achieving policy goals. Toward this end, environmental groups' leaders find it more important to be incorporated, or "close to power," than to "fight" for political goals, particularly since the former is a better fundraising strategy.

The conclusions of Ronald Shaiko's (1999) study of five leading environmental groups are consistent with Dowie's charge. The focus of Shaiko's analysis is the relationship between the leadership of environmental interest groups and their membership. He specifically seeks to understand the ability of the leaders and members to communicate on policy questions. This requires a two-part assessment. First, Shaiko analyzes the extent to which interest group leaders solicit the opinions of their members on various policy questions, and the extent to which institutional mechanisms exist within these organizations that allow members to communicate their policy preferences to the leadership. Second, he analyzes the ability and success of environmental interest groups to mobilize their membership on public policy questions. Shaiko utilizes data from five groups: Sierra Club (SC), The Wilderness Society (TWS), National Wildlife Federation (NWF), Environmental Defense Fund (EDF) (now Environmental Defense [ED]), and Environmental Action (EA). Like Dowie, Shaiko concludes from his analysis that environmental interest group leaders tend to prioritize organizational maintenance over political advocacy.[31]

According to Shaiko, a key reason for the increasing emphasis on organizational maintenance is the public interest group milieu, which during the last forty years has seen a substantial growth in the number of public interest organizations competing for members among a limited pool of individuals who possess the inclination and disposable income to pay membership fees. With an emphasis on organizational maintenance, environmental interest group leaders, to varying degrees, have come to view their members more as an economic constituency and less as a political constituency. This is best exemplified and reinforced by two trends among environmental groups: one, the hiring of individuals from outside the environmental movement to lead environmental interest groups for the specific purpose of organizational maintenance; two, the offering of perks to individuals to join or renew their memberships. Such perks include credit cards, posters, calendars, and magazine subscriptions. Moreover, Shaiko's analysis demonstrates that environmental interest group members tend to join these organizations largely for the tangible perks and less for reasons related to political advocacy and public policy.

Another reason environmental groups would participate in a policy-making process that excludes key issues is that the ecological modernization of urban sprawl would not go forward were it not for the participation of these groups.[32] The belief that lobbying on the part of environmental groups is pushing government to forward the ecological modernization of the automobile, in particular, is reflected in the following NRDC Web site posting:

> In August 2004 we asked California activists to urge the California Air Resources Board [CARB] to adopt strong regulations to reduce global warming pollution from new cars sold in California. You [the public] sent more than 4,000 messages during the board's comment period, and we're thrilled to report that, at its September 2004 meeting in Los Angeles, the board voted unanimously to adopt the strong regulations we supported. The new standards, the first of their kind in the nation, require tailpipe emissions of carbon dioxide and other pollutants that cause global warming to be reduced by 22 percent by 2012 and by 30 percent by 2016. New York and other New England states will probably follow California's lead, and Canada is considering enacting similar standards as well. The auto industry has announced it will challenge the standards in court, so we'll be sure to keep you posted on future developments, but for now the decision stands as a major milestone in the fight to stop global warming—thanks to all of you who helped achieve it![33]

## The Business Community, Urban Sprawl, and Ecological Modernization

The ecological modernization of the U.S. economy has historically been promoted by significant segments of the business community (Gonzalez 2005a). This includes the ecological modernization of the economy to abate greenhouse gases (i.e., the WBCSD and the ICC).

With leading members of the corporate community providing support and energy to political efforts that would ecologically modernize the economy, including urban sprawl, the political contribution of those environmental lobbying activists to the policymaking process becomes unclear. In other words, with important elements of the business community promoting the ecological modernization of the economy, it becomes difficult to determine to what extent environmental activists are advancing the ecological modernization agenda. Hence, those public policies designed to forward the ecological modernization of the internal combustion engine, and the energy infrastructure, could be the result of business political actions, and not those of environmental lobbyists.

Furthermore, determining the actual influence of environmental lobbying efforts is complicated by the fact that, as Dowie (1995, 48) points out, environmental groups, for purposes of fundraising, are apt to take full credit for perceived legislative or regulatory victories even when they do not deserve it. With the federal government abandoning the Kyoto Protocol, as noted in chapter 2, the notion that incorporated environmental groups exercise significant influence over the federal government appears doubtful. The federal government did so in face of strong opposition from the environmental lobbying community (Browne 2002; Lisowski 2002; Hovi, Skodvin, and Andresen 2003). In the case of California, the environmental lobbying community strongly opposed the CARB's retreat from its zero-emission automobile plan (Gonzalez 2005a, ch. 6).

Given the political activity of the WBCSD and the ICC, it becomes apparent that the ecological modernization of the economy to address climate change will go forward with or without the incorporation of environmental activists into the policymaking process. Albeit, this modernization *might* not proceed at the same pace.

## CONCLUSION

In light of the factors described here, the participation of environmental activists in the policymaking process takes on ethical dimensions. We can see that these activists enhance public support for a policy formulation process that primarily abets the agenda of the business community—minimizing/eliminating greenhouse emissions from urban sprawl. They also dampen those political forces (i.e., rebellious politics) that would compel the treatment of questions and issues that are central to a salutary and sustainable environment. Moreover, it is uncertain what environmental activists gain, in terms of environmental protection, for their participation in the policymaking process.

The environmental community as a whole, however, has affected politics, particularly in the realm of public opinion. Environmental ethicist Lester Milbrath (1995) explains that "public opinion polls show that a majority, usually a high majority, of people in most countries are aware of environmental problems and very concerned about getting them solved to ensure a decent future." (102). No doubt, the environmental community deserves at least partial credit for the awareness among the world's citizenry of environmental problems (Desai 2002; Smith 2002; Guber 2003; Banerjee 2008).

This success, along with the dubious nature of their participation within the policy formulation process, would suggest that the most efficacious deployment of the environmental lobbying community's resources would directly involve the public and specifically civil society. As Milbrath explains, environmental "awareness and concern does not necessarily mean that people well understand" the causes and potential solutions to society's environmental ills (1995, 102; also see Bednar 2003). Hence, instead of maintaining a somewhat hostile and contentious attitude toward those confrontational environmental groups and networks that operate outside of the polity (Dowie 1995; Doherty 2002), the environmental lobbying community should exit the polity and join with their rebellious brethren in civil society (Norton 1991). In this way, those resources currently deployed lobbying officials within government could be more fruitfully directed at educating the public about the profoundly negative environmental, economic, and social impacts of urban sprawl (Bullard and Johnson 1997; Hayden 2003; Wolch, Pastor, and Dreir 2004; Johnson and Klemens 2005; Sloman 2006).

For instance, such an education effort might involve informing the public how government agencies, both federal and state, utilize a narrow or "weak" conception of ecological modernization, relying on technological solutions to the problem of climate-changing emissions (Christoff 1996; Neumayer 2003; Dryzek 2005, ch. 8). A more expansive or "stronger" conception of ecological modernization might include, for example, ecologically sensitive land management mandating the intensive usage of land (as opposed to sprawl [Purdum 2000]), the concentration of residential and work areas, and the adoption of mass transit as the primary means of transportation in urban areas. Ecologically sensitive land management would seek to redirect urban residents away from their dependence on the automobile (and the internal combustion engine) and toward more ecologically benign forms of transportation, such as walking, bicycling, and mass transit (Sloman 2006). It would also encourage the construction of smaller abodes that would require less energy consumption (Pinderhughes 2004). Finally, such an education campaign could serve to expand rebellious environmental politics into a social movement that would, potentially, force policymakers to abandon the narrow version of ecological modernization and instead employ the more expansive version of this concept, which would curtail climate-changing emissions, as well as ease traffic congestion, lower transportation costs, and result in more efficient land use.

# Conclusion

## Political Power and the Future of the Planet

As outlined in chapter 1, the globalization thesis and the empire of capital position are two competing approaches to analyzing the operation of the global economy. Advocates of the former hold that states as institutions are less relevant today because of the advances in communication and transportation technologies that have increasingly integrated the world economy. As a result, market forces are the most significant factors in shaping the operation of the global economy. Moreover, political and policymaking power has increasingly shifted to international institutions that help oversee the functioning of the world economy (i.e., the World Bank, the International Monetary Fund, and the World Trade Organization), as well as to the multinational corporations that own/control the global infrastructures of production and the world's marketing and distribution networks.

In contrast, the proponents of the empire of capital position aver that states remain as key institutions in the maintenance and operation of the global economy. In particular, states are central in upholding and enforcing capitalist property relations, whereby workers are legally/politically alienated from the means of production. This alienation allows capitalists to purchase the labor of workers for less than it is worth. Additionally, the states of the advanced capitalist countries are central in maintaining a world economic system that has historically benefited this set of nation-states.

The role of the U.S. state in fostering and maintaining urban sprawl lends support to the empire of capital argument. Because of this sponsoring and encouragement of urban sprawl, major U.S. cities are the most sprawled and the most automobile dependent on the planet. Urban sprawl has a number of positive economic effects. It greatly increases demand for automobiles. Among the world's major cities, those in the United States have by far the highest per capita ownership of automobiles. Moreover, because urban sprawl tends to produce spacious homes on the urban periphery, such sprawl also increases effective demand for consumer durables, such as appliances and furniture, to fill these homes. Finally, urban sprawl increases demand for energy as large amounts of gasoline are required for commuting via automobile, and relatively large amounts of energy are needed to power the appliances that fill spacious homes and to heat/cool these homes. (While comprising less than 5 percent of the world's population, U.S. residents consume about 20 percent of the globe's goods and services.) Today, the U.S. government promotes urban sprawl through land use policies, road building projects, low-cost mortgage programs (e.g., Fannie Mae and Freddie Mac), and sustained efforts to minimize/stabilize oil prices.[1]

As explained in chapter 4, urban sprawl was embraced by policymakers at the national level beginning in the 1930s as a means of profitably absorbing surplus capital and the output of the nation's industrial base—which by the 1920s was increasingly focused on producing consumer durables, including automobiles. So while the techniques of urban sprawl were developed by large landholders and developers during the turn of the twentieth century (chapter 3), these techniques were nationally instituted by the federal government beginning in the 1930s—predominately through the Federal Housing Authority (FHA). The postwar economic boom experienced by the United States can be directly attributed to the nationwide application of the techniques of urban sprawl, and the subsequent sprawling of urban zones throughout the country.

Among the most important pro–urban sprawl policies the federal government has instituted have been its oil policies. As pointed out in chapter 5, through these policies policymakers have sought to maintain oil prices at a level that allows urban sprawl and automobile consumption/use. These policies remained in place even as the automobile dependence, and the subsequent oil dependency, of U.S. urban zones became a glaring liability. The United States' current occupation of Iraq can be viewed as an effort to minimize this liability. The occupation itself highlights the precarious situation the United States is in with regard to oil. The occupation, to date, has devolved into a quagmire, bogging down the U.S. military—absorbing greater and greater amounts of human and monetary resources—without any end in sight. While the occupation has damaged the nation's military ("Military Tells Bush" 2008), international (Shanker 2008 Feb 9), and financial (Stiglitz and Bilmes 2008) standing, a withdrawal without the establishment of a pro-Western Iraqi government is a seeming impossibility (Bohan 2006). The petroleum resources of the Persian Gulf region are simply too vital to the U.S. economy, and as a result to the world economy, for the U.S. military to withdraw from Iraq while the possibility exists that an unstable or anti-West Iraq could destabilize the entire region (Baker 2006; Marsh 2006).

A key question for political scientists is, What factors have prompted the policies that promote/foster urban sprawl in the United States? In chapter 2, I put forward two competing policymaking approaches to analyze the political factors that have historically determined the pro–urban sprawl policies of the U.S. government. These approaches are entitled state autonomy theory and economic elite theory. The first emphasizes the ability of officials within the state to formulate and implement public policies independently of societal groups, including business interests. Additionally, these officials often draw policy ideas from different groups, experts, and perspectives. In this way, environmental groups and their views are often incorporated into the policymaking process.

In contrast to the state autonomy approach, economic elite theory stresses the role of economic elites in policy formulation. These elites exercise dominant influence over the state because they possess ample wealth and income, which can be converted into a number of useful and advantageous political tools: campaign finance, publicity, access, etc. Moreover, economic elites operate through policy-planning organizations, which supply them with information, analysis, and the means to build a consensus on proposed policies among elites in general. Through such organizations, economic elites can determine and agree upon those policies that are going to enhance their market positions and improve the overall operation of the economy.

In turning to the empirical record, it becomes evident that the economic elite approach offers deeper insight into the development of pro–urban sprawl policies than the state autonomy approach. The techniques of urban sprawl were disseminated throughout the U.S. real estate industry during the early twentieth century through the policy-planning organizations of the Home Builders and Subdividers Division and the City Planning Committee of the National Association of Real Estate Boards—both of which were led by large land developers.

Additionally, political efforts to institute the techniques of urban sprawl nationwide were initiated in the 1930s by the Committee on Finance of the President's Conference on Home Building and Home Ownership, and the President's Emergency Committee on Housing. The committee on finance was made up of leading figures within the U.S. financial community, and the committee's recommendations focused on how to make domestic real estate a more stable and profitable investment opportunity. In this way, domestic real estate could serve to profitably absorb U.S. capital, which could no longer be invested in Europe or the equity market. The policy recommendations of this committee were adopted by the FHA in its pro–urban sprawl efforts.

The President's Emergency Committee on Housing was made up in part of important figures from the business community, most significantly

W. Averell Harriman (a partner of Brown Harriman, a leading New York investment firm), an assistant to Alfred Sloan (the president and chairperson of General Motors), and the chairperson of the Federal Home Loan Bank Board. The presence of Sloan on this committee is especially noteworthy, since the automobile sector had long made it its political objective to create automobile dependency. The intent of the President's Emergency Committee on Housing was to increase the consumption of consumer durables through an expanded housing market. The work of the committee led directly to the creation of the FHA. The FHA was, in turn, populated with individuals from the real estate industry who were directly involved with applying the techniques of sprawl. As a result, the FHA formulated and implemented policies that served as major impetuses to the sprawling of urban America.

In order to maintain the low oil prices necessary for urban sprawl, during the post–World War II era the United States sought to include the major oil-bearing regions outside of the Soviet Union within its sphere of influence. This foreign policy was laid out by the Council on Foreign Relation's (CFR) War and Peace Studies project during World War II. The CFR is a policy-planning organization financed and led by economic elites. The CFR War and Peace Studies project's recommendations served as the basis of postwar U.S. foreign policy. A central recommendation put forward by the project members was the "Grand Area" concept. According to the proponents of this concept, the American economy must have access to certain portions of the world to properly operate. Within this grand area proposed by the CFR were all of the known oil bearing regions of the world outside of the Soviet Union—including the Persian Gulf.

Two other economic elite policy-planning groups that were influential in shaping post–World War II foreign oil policy were the Petroleum Administrator of War's Foreign Oil Committee and the Petroleum Industry War Council—both of which were made up of executives from the U.S. petroleum industry. For their part, the Foreign Oil Committee and the Petroleum Industry War Council advised during the war that U.S. foreign oil policy should be geared toward gaining access to the world's sources of petroleum for U.S. oil firms. In doing so, these organizations defeated the Petroleum Reserve Corporation plan, which had been initiated within the state during World War II. This plan was designed to bring foreign supplies of oil under U.S. government control, thereby allowing state officials to switch the focus of the U.S. energy economy from domestic petroleum production to those foreign oil sources controlled by the U.S. government. The intended result was the conservation of domestic supplies of U.S. crude.

The depletion of U.S. oil stocks throughout the postwar period dramatically raised the importance of Persian Gulf petroleum production for the U.S. economy. This importance/dependency came into sharp relief with the short-lived oil embargo instituted by Saudi Arabia in 1973. Even in the aftermath of the severe petroleum shortfalls that resulted from the 1973 and 1979 oil shocks, however, the United States maintained its liberal oil consumption policy. Instead of addressing U.S. vulnerability to oil and the Persian Gulf region by curbing domestic oil consumption, the federal government intensified its military and diplomatic efforts to ensure the flow of petroleum from the Persian Gulf. As explained in chapter 5, this supply-side answer to the 1970s oil crises is consistent with the advice put forward in the mid-1970s by the Twentieth Century Fund's task forces on "U.S. Energy Policy" and the "International Oil Crisis." Both of these were economic elite policy-planning groups. The key recommendation offered by these groups to alleviate the high oil prices of the 1970s was to cultivate sources of petroleum outside of the OPEC countries. Another recommendation of the task force on U.S. energy policy was to improve the efficiency of the economy's energy consumption, especially in regard to gasoline use. It is significant, however, that neither task force counseled less driving or lowering the automobile dependency of U.S. urban areas to reduce oil prices and reduce the strategic advantage of the OPEC countries.

While the urban sprawl policies of the United States can be credited with fostering global economic growth and stability, urban sprawl has two significant liabilities: climate change and oil depletion. Both of these liabilities result directly from the fact that urban sprawl is predicated on the profligate utilization of fossil fuels. As a result, greenhouse gases, especially carbon dioxide, are being emitted into the atmosphere at a rate that cannot be safely absorbed by the biosphere. Because of this the planet is warming and the oceans are becoming acidic at alarming rates. With the United States having the most sprawled urban zones in the world, unsurprisingly it is at least the second-largest collective emitter of carbon dioxide (with China, perhaps, recently surpassing the United States as the world's leading absolute source [Rosenthal 2008 June 14]), and per capita the United States leads virtually all nations.[2]

Fossil fuels are the most readily available and abundant sources of potential energy on the planet. Nevertheless, they are finite. At current rates of consumption, peak production of the fossil fuel petroleum is set to occur in the near future (if it has not already occurred). This is a particular threat to those cities that are highly sprawled and automobile dependent, because there is no readily available alternative to gasoline/diesel that is economically viable.

With urban sprawl accelerating both climate change and oil depletion, environmentalists and conservationists should make reforming U.S. urban zones their top priority. Since the public policymaking process generally excludes any questioning of urban sprawl, those interested in abating climate-changing emissions and oil use should withdraw from this process. By doing so, they would cease to enhance the legitimacy of the policymaking process. Moreover, given the outlook and activity of the World Business Council for Sustainable Development and the International Chamber of Commerce (both of which are economic elite policy-planning groups), the "weak" ecological modernization of the U.S. energy and transportation infrastructures will go forward with or without the inclusion of environmental groups in the state's policymaking process.

Those interested in decisively reforming the treatment of the environment and the current rate of natural resource depletion should, ideally, embark on an effort to educate the public about how key questions and issues are excluded from the public policymaking process. Such an education effort might spark a social movement that would prompt the reforming of U.S. urban areas onto the political agenda. As noted in chapter 6, there are already grassroots groups and community organizations that focus on the significant economic and social costs created by the sprawled quality of U.S. urban zones.

Given the recent tightening of petroleum supplies and the very definite possibility of global oil production peaking in the immediate future, it is imperative that the automobile dependence of U.S. urban zones be politically contested. This is because the most likely current replacements for petroleum-derived fuels are fuels drawn from tar sands, oil shale, and coal. (The U.S. Air Force is already aggressively researching liquefying coal as a substitute for oil-based jet fuel [Philips 2007].) Using liquid fuels from these sources of energy on a large scale would release massive additional amounts of carbon into the biosphere (Roberts 2004; Leggett 2005; Motavalli 2006; Wald 2006).

In challenging urban sprawl, questions are going to be raised about whether the global economy can exist as we know it with a post–urban sprawl U.S. society. Of course, global warming and oil depletion should already prompt such questions.[3] The only real issue is, Are we going to confront these questions before or after a permanent and disastrous petroleum shortfall occurs, or before or after we have pumped so much carbon dioxide and other greenhouse gases into the air (Campbell 2008; Diaz and Murname 2008; Volk 2008) that life as we know it is unsustainable on Earth?

# Notes

## Chapter One. Urban Sprawl and the Empire of Capital

1. According to the Netherlands Environmental Assessment Agency, China in 2007 surpassed the United States as the largest absolute emitter of carbon dioxide (Rosenthal 2008 June 14).

2. There are six small countries that emit more carbon dioxide than the United States on a per capita basis: Qatar, Luxembourg, Netherlands Antilles, United Arab Emirates, Kuwait, and Bahrain (International Energy Agency 2007, Part Two, 49–51).

3. A 2004 study conducted in the Atlanta metropolitan area found that detached single-family homes consumed 23 percent more energy than attached single-family homes, and 68 percent more energy than homes located in multifamily structures (i.e., apartment complexes) (Williams 2008).

4. Ewing et al. (2007), Burchell (2005), Solecki and Oliveri (2004), Jianguo Liu et al. (2003), and MacKellar et al. (1995) treat the positive relationship between urban sprawl and climate change gas emissions.

5. To this point, Manuel Castells (1996/1998) adds that in the modern economy ideas (i.e., intellectual property) and information are serving as increasing sources of wealth accumulation. As a result, the state, as the sole enforcer of property relations (including in the areas of ideas and information), increases in importance in the global process of capital accumulation (also see Braman 2006).

6. With comparatively high automotive usage, in 1990 the U.S. cities studied had the highest per capita emission of carbon dioxide resulting from private transportation—4,609 kilograms. The Australian cities emitted 2,774 kilograms per capita; Canada, 2,675; Europe, 1,769; wealthy Asian cities, 997; and developing Asian cities, 739. When diesel powered and electric powered forms of transportation are factored in, the total per capita emissions of carbon dioxide were in 1990: United States, 4,683; Australia, 2,883; Canada, 2,764; Europe, 1,887; wealthy Asian cities, 1,158; and developing Asian cities, 837. These data indicate that for all the cities studied private forms of transportation powered by gasoline

113

combustion engines (e.g., automobiles, vans, buses, and midsized trucks) are the primary source of carbon dioxide emanating from transportation. In the case of the United States, for instance, diesel (e.g., commercial trucks and public buses) and electrically powered (e.g., subways) forms of transportation only contributed 74 kilograms of carbon dioxide emissions per capita (Kenworthy and Laube 1999, 603).

7. The per capita emission of carbon dioxide in 2004 for the countries listed in Table 1.4 were: United States, 19.7 tons; Russia, 10.6 tons; Germany, 10.3; South Korea, 9.65; Japan, 9.4; United Kingdom, 9.0; France, 6.2; China, 3.5; and India, 1.0 (International Energy Agency 2007, Part Two, 49–51).

8. DeCicco and Fung (2006) report that in 2000 automobile usage (including light trucks) in the United States resulted in 45 percent of total global automotive climate change emissions (2).

# Chapter Two. Political Economy and the Imperatives of the State

1. The concept of political economy that informs my argument is one that views economic systems as political systems (Block 1990; Roy 1997). This is because economic systems historically privilege certain values and interests, often at the expense of other values and interests. Capitalism—of particular relevance to this study—prioritizes profit and the interests of the capitalist class (i.e., the economic elite), often at the expense of workers and the environment (Gorz 1994; Perelman 2003). In this instance, the question is, Who economically/politically benefits from the public policies promoting urban sprawl, and how?

2. I offer a full description of this model elsewhere (2001a, 10–13), so here I will only provide its central features. It merits noting that Almond (1988) contends that the claim of originality made by state autonomy theorists is unwarranted, since autonomous state officials have been an explicit aspect of pluralist theory from its inception.

3. Barrow (1993) explains that "corporations emerged as the dominant economic institutions in capitalist societies by the end of the nineteenth century." He goes on to note that as early as the late 1920s "the bulk of U.S. economic activity, whether measured in terms of assets, profits, employment, investment, market shares, or research and development, was concentrated in the fifty largest financial institutions and five hundred largest nonfinancial corporations" (17).

4. The economic elite–led policy-planning network has two groupings—one that is characterized as "moderate" or "corporate liberal" and the other as "conservative." While these two groups will frequently compromise on

issues, they sometimes cannot. When they cannot find common ground, their struggles will usually spill over into government where each will utilize its political strength to try and get its way (Weinstein 1968, ch. 1; Eakins 1969, 1972; Domhoff 1978a, ch. 3; 1990, 38–39; Barrow 1993, ch. 1).

5. Several of the union representatives on CCEEB's board are from the building trades, which have historically been strong proponents of local growth (Logan and Molotch 1987, 81–82). Moreover, many of the private citizens on its board were former corporate executives. One, for example, had been a vice- president of Bank of America (Weisser 2000). None of CCEEB's board members are leaders from the environmental community.

## Chapter Three. Real Estate Interests and the Techniques of Urban Sprawl

1. The one business group in Chicago, and other urban areas, that looked negatively upon urban sprawl were downtown interests, who saw sprawl as undermining their position as the center of commerce for the city (Fogelson 2001).

## Chapter Four. The Federal Government and the National Establishment of Urban Sprawl

1. Historian T. C. Barker (1985), in the following, reports on automobile ownership during the 1930s among the leading economies of the world at the time:

> There were then [1939] only 2,000,000 cars of all makes registered in the whole country [of Great Britain] (and 460,000 motor cycles), while the United States, with less than three times the population, possessed 30,000,000 cars. And Britain was well ahead of the other Europeans. France, for instance, had only 1,600,000 cars in 1938 and Germany, still at an earlier stage of market growth, had fewer: 1,100,000 cars (and 1,300,000 motor cycles). (6)

2. This Board headed up the Federal Home Loan Bank System, created in 1932. It was made up of eleven regionally based home loan banks that served as a central credit agency similar to the Federal Reserve System.

3. General Motors' presence on a government housing committee seeking the expansion of consumer durables consumption contradicts economic historian Elliot Rosen's (2005) claim that during the Great Depression "there is scant evidence, if any, that automobile producers, the nation's

principal industry, sought government intervention." Rosen goes on to assert "here [in the automobile industry] the market was permitted to operate unimpeded and unaided" (118).

4. Most automobiles in the 1920s were purchased through credit. Nonetheless, as consumer credit historian Lendol Caldwell (1999) explains "throughout the 1920s 25 to 40 percent of Americans in any given year continued to buy cars for cash" (194). The terms of retail automotive credit were rather stringent during the 1920s. Loan terms required one-third of the purchase price upon signing, and the amortization period on automobile loans was between six and twelve months. Moreover, economic historian Martha Olney (1989) reports that the "effective annual interest rate exceeded 30 percent" on automobiles purchased through credit in the 1920s (381). In the 1930s automotive credit terms were substantially liberalized. A general liberalization occurred in the 1930s on terms of credit with regard to the purchase of consumer durables (Calder 1999, 275).

# Chapter Five. U.S. Oil Policy and Urban Sprawl

1. In 1975, in response to the oil shock of 1973, the U.S. government established the Strategic Petroleum Reserve program (Beaubouef 2007).

2. In a 1969 profile of Walter J. Levy, entitled "As Oil Consultant, He's Without Like or Equal," the *New York Times* noted that "he is readily acknowledged as the 'dean of oil consultants' even by competitors." The profile went on to explain that "there are few, if any, major oil controversies in which Mr. Levy has not acted as a consultant," and that he "has been an advisor to most of the major oil companies, most of the important consuming countries and many of the large producing countries" ("As Oil Consultant" 1969).

3. According to the U.S. Energy Information Administration, global petroleum production in 2005 was 83.7 million barrels per day. According to the United States Department of Energy, in 2005 the United States consumed 9.1 million barrels per day of petroleum equivalent on powering automobiles (including light trucks and motorcycles) (United States Department of Energy, Table 2.6; Energy Information Administration, Table 5.1).

4. In 2006 U.S. petroleum consumption was estimated at 20.6 million barrels per day, whereas global petroleum production in 2006 was close to 84.8 million barrels per day (Energy Information Administration 2008, Figure 5). Of these 20.6 million barrels per day of U.S. consumption, 68 percent (14 million barrels per day) went toward transportation: automobiles, buses, aircraft, ships, and trains. Of the entire total, 44 percent (9 million barrels per day) went toward producing "motor gasoline." Another 3 mil-

lion barrels per day went toward producing distillate fuel oil, which includes diesel fuel. Diesel fuel is used to power automobiles and buses, as well as heavy and medium trucks (Energy Information Administration 2007, Table 5.1 and 5.13c; Duffield 2008, 19).

5. Between 1981 and 1986, U.S. daily consumption of petroleum increased by 120,000 barrels, whereas Western European consumption dropped 490,000 barrels (Philip 1994, 195).

6. Nersesian (2007) notes that the United States, Colombia, Egypt, Indonesia, and the United Kingdom have all reached peak petroleum production, and oil extraction in these countries is in a steady decline (199). Despite Hubbert's success in modeling U.S. oil production and the apparent peaking of petroleum extraction in major producing countries, the U.S. government officially denies the validity of Hubbert's theory. Moreover, prominent officials in the petroleum industry also dispute it (Goodstein 2004; Roberts 2004; "World Oil Demand to Peak Before Supply" 2008).

7. An alternative argument to explain the recent spike in petroleum prices points to the recent merger of oil companies. This merger trend has resulted in fewer overall oil firms, which facilitates their ability to manipulate prices (Blas, Boxell, and Morrison 2005).

8. The drop in the price of petroleum in the latter half of 2008 was due to a decline in global demand (Krauss 2008 Oct. 14).

# Chapter 6. Democratic Ethics, Ecological Modernization, and Symbolic Inclusion

1. In its budget for the fiscal year 2009 the Bush administration dropped the planned financing of a coal-fired power plant designed to capture and sequester carbon dioxide emissions (Mufson 2008).

2. Biofuels are fuels derived from plant or organic materials. Studies have found that increased biofuel use would likely increase overall carbon dioxide atmospheric levels. This is because a surge in biofuel production/consumption would lead to an increase in the clearing of wilderness (e.g., rainforest and savannah) to produce more biofuel source materials (e.g., sugar, corn, and soybean), or to replace lands lost to food production as a result of expanded ethanol creation. Wilderness is a key carbon sink. Moreover, the destruction of wilderness to meet increased ethanol demand is predicted to elevate carbon dioxide emissions, as the burning/decomposing of cleared wilderness debris emits large amounts of carbon dioxide (Rosenthal 2008 Feb. 8).

3. Hundreds of towns have joined the United States Conference of Mayors Climate Protection Agreement—"pledging to meet the Kyoto standards for carbon emissions by 2012" (Williams 2008).

4. Sierra Club, "Global Warming & Energy: Overview: Solutions." Available at http://www.sierraclub.org/globalwarming/overview/solutions. asp (viewed 2008 February 16).

5. NRDC (Natural Resources Defense Council), "Global Warming Basics What It Is, How It's Caused, and What Needs to Be Done to Stop It." http://www.nrdc.org/globalWarming/f101.asp#7 (viewed 2008 February 16).

6. I sought out the positions of four environmental groups that lobby in Washington, D.C., on the issue of climate change: NRDC, the Sierra Club, UCS, and U.S. PIRG. I focused on these four groups because in my informal telephone conversations with Washington, D.C.–based environmental group officials they were listed as the most visible and active groups in lobbying in Washington, D.C., on climate change. This is especially the case as it relates to issues of automobiles and energy. All four of these groups have lobbying offices in Washington, DC.

7. Sierra Club, "Global Warming & Energy: Overview: Solutions." In 2007, the Natural Resources Defense Council, along with Environmental Defense, the World Resources Institute, and the Pew Center on Global Climate Change, formed the United States Climate Action Partnership with ten major businesses: Dupont; General Electric; Alcoa; Caterpillar; Duke Energy; PG&E of California; the FPL Group of Florida; PNM Resources of New Mexico; British Petroleum; and Lehman Brothers. The political goal of the partnership is to reduce climate-changing emissions through the development and deployment of energy-efficient and abatement technologies (Barringer 2007 Jan. 19).

8. UCS (Union of Concerned Scientists), "Global Warming Solutions." http://www.ucsusa.org/global_warming/solutions/ (viewed 2008 February 20).

9. I sought extensive interviews with four environmental organizations: the Union of Concerned Scientists, Sierra Club, U.S. PIRG, and the Natural Resources Defense Council. In informal discussions with officials from Washington, D.C.-based environmental groups these four were commonly listed as the most visible on the issues of climate change, transportation, and energy. (Environmental Defense was also mentioned, but, for reasons discussed in note 13, I did not pursue an interview with this organization.) After repeated telephone and e-mail messages throughout May, June, and July of 2005, I was only able to interview the climate change lobbyist for the Union of Concerned Scientists. I want to take this opportunity to express my gratitude for her time and openness.

10. U.S. PIRG, "Stopping Global Warming Pollution." http://uspirg. org/uspirg.asp?id2=23978 (viewed 2008 February 16).

11. Natural Resources Defense Council (NRDC), "Solving Global Warming." http://www.nrdc.org/globalWarming/solutions/step2.asp (viewed 2008 February 16).

12. NRDC, "Global Warming Basics What It Is."

13. Environmental Defense was also mentioned as an environmental organization visible and active on the issues of climate change, transportation, and energy in Washington, D.C. I did not discuss their Web site here nor pursue an interview with one of their officials because they are not an "oppositional" group, as outlined by Dryzek. Environmental Defense embraces the prime aspects of the U.S. economy, and instead makes it its key political goal to reform the U.S. economy at the margins (Dowie 1995, 108).

14. GCC (Global Climate Coalition), "About Us: What Is the GCC." Formerly available at http://www.globalclimate.org/aboutus.htm (viewed 2004 February 20).

15. Ibid.

16. WBCSD (World Business Council for Sustainable Development), "About the WBCSD." Available at http://www.wbcsd.org (viewed 2008 Feb. 15).

17. Ibid.

18. Ibid. (viewed 2004 Feb. 20).

19. Studies have found that increased biofuel use would likely increase overall carbon dioxide levels in the atmosphere. This is because a surge in biofuel production/consumption will lead to an increase in the clearing of wilderness (e.g., rainforest and savannah) to produce more ethanol source materials (e.g., sugar, corn, and soybean), or to replace lands lost to food production as a result of expanded ethanol creation. Wilderness is a key carbon sink, and its destruction would undermine the carbon cycle and inhibit the storage of carbon in a benign form. Moreover, the destruction of wilderness to meet increased ethanol demand is predicted to elevate carbon dioxide emissions, as the burning/decomposing of cleared wilderness debris emits large amounts of carbon dioxide (Rosenthal 2008 Feb. 8).

20. In a 2005 document titled *Pathways to 2050: Energy and Climate*, the World Business Council for Sustainable Development (WBCSD) renders its vision on energy use and climate change emissions through to 2050. On the issue of "Mobility," throughout the years until 2045 the WBCSD counsels the use of biomass, hydrogen, hybrids, and diesel. Only "by 2050" does the WBCSD predict "a further shift to mass transportation," which "offers considerable efficiency benefits." "By 2050" the WBCSD (2005) foresees that "substantial investments are made worldwide to make this an efficient and attractive alternative to individual transport" (8–9).

Similarly, in a 2004 WBCSD report titled *Mobility 2030: Meeting the Challenge of Sustainability* (authored by executives from General Motors, Toyota, Shell Oil, British Petroleum, DaimlerChrysler, Ford, Honda, Michelin Tire Company, Nissan Motor, Norsk Hydro, Renault, and Volkswagen), the following observation is offered:

Over the very long run—*five decades or more*—societies face a fundamental choice about how their mobility patterns will develop. Some hold that in order to make mobility sustainable, people will have to be induced to live in significantly more dense agglomerations. According to this view, only by doing this will it be technologically and financially feasible to rely on public transport to a much greater degree than is generally the case today. (emphasis added)

In opposition to those who champion efficient land use and greatly expanded public mass transit, the authors of *Mobility 2030* declare:

To us, this strategy seems to rest on forcing people to adapt to the technological and economic characteristics of transport systems. An alternative strategy is to adapt the technological and economic characteristics of transport systems to fit the living choices of the public. The various vehicle technologies we have described [throughout the *Mobility 2030* report] appear to have the potential to enable such an adaptation. (25)

21. For a comprehensive discussion of the economic and environmental shortcomings of alternative fuels and carbon sequestration technologies see Roberts 2004; Heinberg 2005.

22. ICC (International Chamber of Commerce), "ICC Membership." Available at http://www.iccwbo.org/id97/index.html (viewed 2008 February 15).

23. Ibid.

24. ICC (International Chamber of Commerce), "How ICC Works." Available at www.iccwbo.org/id96/index.html (viewed 2008 February 15).

25. ICC (International Chamber of Commerce) Commission on Environment and Energy, "Leadership." Available at http://www.iccwbo.org/policy/environment/id1456/index.html (viewed 2008 February 15).

26. In response to rising energy prices, the ICC's Commission on Environment and Energy put out in May 2007 a policy statement titled "Energy Security: A Worldwide Business Perspective." The authors of this policy statement aver that "research offers the promise of innovative technologies that promote energy security, for example, through efficiency gains and diversification of energy supply sources." They go on to add "strong long-term energy technology research, development and deployment should be pursued by both government and industry in the pursuit of more sustainable future energy system." Finally, the authors of "Energy Security" confidently assert that "advancements in technology will continue to improve global energy security, and will also lessen the impact of energy-related activities on the environment" (5).

Also expressed in this document is the view that the role of governments in a tight energy market is not to promote conservation. Instead, "Governments have a role . . . in providing incentives to conduct [energy-related] research," and "through education and capacity building in universities to maintain the supply chain of well-trained scientists and engineers." Moreover, "Governments can also enhance the ability of markets to deploy new [energy] technologies through investment and technology transfer" (5).

27. The current alternative fuel automobile plan put forward by CARB mandates that automotive firms in aggregate make available for sale in California 250 hydrogen fuel cell–powered vehicles between the 2005 and 2008 model years; 2,500 from 2009 to 2011; and 25,000 from 2012 to 2014. Firms can comply with these aggregate targets with battery powered vehicles (Hakim 2003 April 25).

28. In addition to the overtly political factors outlined here, psychological, cultural, and ideological barriers exist that prevent a more robust and confrontational politics arising from civil society to challenge the state's commitment to environmentally deleterious growth (Milbrath 1989, 1995, 1996; Cahn 1995; Bednar 2003).

29. When the 2007 energy law was passed corporate average fuel efficiency [CAFE] standards for automobiles and light trucks were 27.5 and 22.5, respectively.

30. As I have already explained, the definition of democracy I am utilizing here emphasizes the ability to consider an indeterminate number of policy goals and means. Another definition of democracy could focus on the procedure through which officials are chosen. In this approach to democracy, as long as central policymakers are democratically elected, then the policy outcomes of their decisions are legitimate and inherently democratic. This legitimacy would extend to those policymakers appointed by the democratically elected officials. Thus, as democratically elected and legally appointed officials, they are justified in excluding certain philosophical and policy perspectives from the policymaking process. This is because these officials can legitimately claim that they speak for the majority of citizens.

The proponents of the former version of democracy would retort that the electoral process in most cases in and of itself does not necessitate or justify elected officials from eliminating policy options from the policymaking process. Instead, many of these theorists hold that U.S. society's reliance on the market to produce and distribute goods and services results in the effective elimination of various policy options from the policymaking process (Lindblom 1982; Barrow 1993, ch. 2; Aronowitz and Bratsis 2002; Bednar 2003). Other thinkers hold that certain policy options are not considered in the policymaking process because particular political and economic interests are able to block their consideration (Bachrach and Baratz 1962; Barrow 1993, ch. 1; Hayward 2000; Wolbrecht and Hero 2005).

31. Among the environmental interest groups that Shaiko examines in detail, it is the ED that most overtly takes the position that its membership is primarily, if not exclusively, an economic resource for its leadership. While the NWF does not openly embrace ED's view of leadership-member relations, it nonetheless limits its political communications to its members for fear of alienating existing and potential dues-paying members. The NWF by far has the largest membership among environmental groups (Shaiko 1999, 41). Among the groups that Shaiko studied, EA was the most active in seeking to mobilize its membership to affect political change. Significantly, EA historically maintained a relatively small membership base, and in 1996 went defunct due to insufficient financial resources. The SC and TWS make more concerted efforts to communicate to its membership on political issues than either the ED or the NWF. Additionally, the SC maintains an institutional mechanism to allow its members to communicate to the group's leaders on issues of public policy. Shaiko nonetheless concludes that in the contemporary period the leaders of these groups prioritize organizational maintenance over political efficacy (Gonzalez 2000).

32. In a June 9, 2005, press release, however, the Natural Resources Defense Council bitterly complained that "in the end, it really won't matter if the Senate passes an energy bill that is marginally better than the one passed by the House. Why are we playing on the margins? Neither bill, so far, comes close to taking us where we need to go. Period."

33. NRDC (Natural Resources Defense Council). http://www.nrdc.org/action/results04.asp (viewed 2008 February 20).

## Conclusion

1. Through Fannie Mae and Freddie Mac the federal government purchases trillions of dollars of mortgage notes from banks and other lenders, thereby freeing up more money to be loaned for home purchases.

2. There are six small countries that emite more carbon dioxide than the United States on a per capita basis: Qatar, Luxembourg, Netherlands Antilles, United Arab Emirates, Kuwait, and Bahrain (International Energy Agency 2007, Part Two, 49–51).

3. For a general discussion on how ecological factors, including pollution emissions, climate change, and resource depletion, undermine the viability/stability of global capitalism see O'Connor 1998; Burkett 1999; Clark and York 2005. Conversely, Bjorn Lomborg (2001, 2007) avers that global capitalism has only marginally degraded the environment. This includes the question of global warming.

# References

*A documentary history of the Petroleum Reserves Corporation, 1943–1944: Prepared for the use of Subcommittee on Multinational Corporations of the Committee on Foreign Relations, United States Senate.* 1974, May 8. Washington, DC: U.S. Government Printing Office.

A faith-based fuel initiative. 2007, January 30. *New York Times*, A20.

Abbott, Carl. 1987. *The new urban America: Growth and politics in Sunbelt cities.* Chapel Hill: University of North Carolina Press.

———. 2008. *How cities won the West: Four centuries of urban change in Western North America.* Albuquerque: University of New Mexico Press.

Abramson, Rudy. 1992. *Spanning the century: The life of W. Averell Harriman, 1891–1986.* New York: William Morrow.

Acher, Robin. 2001. Does repression help to create labor parties? The effect of police and military intervention on unions in the United States and Australia. *Studies in American Political Development* 15 (Fall): 189–219.

———. 2008. *Why is there no Labor Party in the United States?* Princeton: Princeton University Press.

Adams, Sean Patrick. 2006. Promotion, competition, captivity: The political economy of coal. *Journal of Policy History* 18, no. 1: 74–95.

Adler, Jonathan H. 1992. Clean fuels, dirty air. In *Environmental politics: Public costs, private rewards*, ed. Michael S. Grave and Fred L. Smith Jr. New York: Praeger.

Agnew, John. 2005. *Hegemony: The new shape of global power.* Philadelphia: Temple University Press.

Agyeman, Julian. 2005. *Sustainable communities and the challenge of environmental justice.* New York: New York University Press.

Agyeman, Julian, Robert D. Bullard, and Bob Evans, eds. 2003. *Just sustainabilities: Development in an unequal world.* Cambridge: MIT Press.

Air Pollution Foundation. 1961. *Final report.* San Marino, CA: Air Pollution Foundation.

Allen, Paul C. 2000. *Phillip III and the Pax Hispanica.* New Haven: Yale University Press.

Almond, Gabriel A. 1988. The return to the state. *American Political Science Review* 82, no. 3: 853–74.

American Petroleum Institute. 1959. *Petroleum facts and figures: Centennial edition.* New York: American Petroleum Institute.

American Road Congress. 1911. *Papers, addresses, and resolutions before the American Road Congress, Richmond, Virginia, November 20–23, 1911.* Baltimore: Waverly Press.

Anderson, Julie M. 2005, July 13. Washington representative (specializing in climate change), Union of Concerned Scientists. Interviewed by author, Washington, DC. Tape recording.

Anderson, Terry L., and Donald R. Leal. 2001. *Free market environmentalism.* New York: Palgrave.

Andrews, Edmund L. 2005, May 21. Greenspan is concerned about "froth" in housing. *New York Times*, C1.

Andrews, Edmund L., and Felicity Barringer. 2007, Jan. 24. Bush seeks vast, mandatory increase in alternative fuels and greater vehicle efficiency. *New York Times*, A1.

Andrews, Edmund L., and Larry Rohter. 2007, March 3. U.S. and Brazil seek to promote ethanol in West. *New York Times*, A1.

Anti-Kyoto industry group folds. Chemical Week, sec. Newsbriefs, the Week, 5.

Armand, Louis. 1955. *Some aspects of the European energy problem: Suggestions for collective action.* Paris: Organization for European Cooperation.

Aronowitz, Stanley, and Peter Bratsis, eds. 2002. *Paradigm lost: State theory reconsidered.* Minneapolis: University of Minnesota Press.

As oil consultant, he's without like or equal. 1969, July 27. *New York Times*, sec. 3, p.3.

Atkinson, Robert D. 2004. *The past and future of America's economy: Long waves of innovation that power cycles of growth.* Northampton, MA: Edward Elgar.

Avila, Eric. 2004. Popular culture in the age of white flight: Film noir, Disneyland, and the cold war (sub)urban imaginary. *Journal of Urban History* 31, no. 1: 3–22.

Avilés, William. 2006. *Global capitalism, democracy, and civil/military relations in Colombia.* Albany: State University of New York Press.

Bacevich, Andrew J. 2005. *The new American militarism: How Americans are seduced by war.* New York: Oxford University Press.

Bachrach, Peter, and Morton Baratz. 1962. Two faces of power. *American Political Science Review* 56, no. 4: 947–52.

Baker, Peter. 2006, Nov. 5. Bush says U.S. pullout would let Iraq radicals use oil as a weapon. *Washington Post*, A6.

Banerjee, Neela. 2008, June 24. Survey of Religion in U.S. finds a broad tolerance for other faiths. *New York Times*, A15.

Banister, David. 2005. *Unsustainable transport: City transport in the new century.* New York: Routledge.

Banister, David, Dominic Stead, Peter Steen, Jonas Åkerman, Karl Dreborg, Peter Nijkamp, and Ruggero Schleicher-Tappeser. 2000. *European transport policy and sustainable mobility.* New York: Spon Press.

Banks, Ferdinand E. 1980. *The political economy of oil.* Lexington, MA: Lexington Books.

———. 1995. *The political economy of coal*. Lexington, MA: Lexington Books.

Barach, Arnold B., and the Twentieth Century Fund. 1964. *USA and its economic future: A Twentieth Century Fund survey*. New York: Macmillan.

Bardhan, Pranab, Samuel Bowles, and Michael Wallerstein, eds. 2006. *Globalization and Egalitarian Redistribution*. Princeton: Princeton University Press.

Bardou, Jean-Pierre, Jean-Jacques Chanaron, Patrick Fridenson, and James M. Laux. 1982. *The automobile revolution: The impact of an industry*. Chapel Hill: University of North Carolina Press.

Barkawi, Tarak. 2006. *Globalization and war*. Lanham, MD: Rowman and Littlefield.

Barker, T. C. 1985. The international history of motor transport. *Journal of Contemporary History* 20, no. 1: 3–19.

Barrett, Paul. 1983. *The automobile and urban transit*. Philadelphia: Temple University Press.

Barrett, Rick. 2007, March 6. Ethanol advocates use Brazil as model. *Milwaukee Journal Sentinel*, D1.

Barringer, Felicity. 2005, Feb. 6. Paper sets off a debate on environmentalism's future. *New York Times*, sec. 1, 18.

———. 2006, Jan. 23. U.S. ranks 28th on environment, a new study says. *New York Times*, A3.

———. 2006, Sept. 15. California, taking big gamble, tries to curb greenhouse gases. *New York Times*, A1.

———. 2007, Jan. 19. A coalition for firm limit on emissions. *New York Times*, C1.

———. 2007, Dec. 21. E.P.A. ruling puts California in a bind. *New York Times*, A37.

———. 2008, Feb. 7. In many communities, it's not easy going green." *New York Times*, A18.

———. 2008, Aug. 29. California moves on bill to curb sprawl and emissions. *New York Times*, A12.

———. 2008, Oct. 20. Green policies in California generated jobs, study finds. *New York Times*, B2.

Barringer, Mark. 2002. *Selling Yellowstone: Capitalism and the construction of nature*. Lawrence: University of Kansas Press.

Barrow, Clyde W. 1990. *Universities and the capitalist state: Corporate liberalism and the reconstruction of American higher education, 1894–1928*. Madison: University of Wisconsin Press.

———. 1992. Corporate liberalism, finance hegemony, and central state intervention in the reconstruction of American higher education. *Studies in American Political Development* 6 (Fall): 420–44.

———. 1993. *Critical theories of the state*. Madison: University of Wisconsin Press.

———. 1998. State theory and the dependency principle: An institutionalist critique of the business climate concept. *Journal of Economic Issues* 32, no. 1: 107–44.

———. 2005. The return of the state: Globalization, state theory, and the new imperialism. *New Political Science* 27, no. 2: 123–45.

Bartik, Timothy J. 1991. *Who benefits from state and local economic development policies?* Kalamazoo, MI: W. E. Upjohn Institute.

Baum-Snow, Nathaniel. 2005. The effects of changes in the transportation infrastructure on suburbanization: Evidence from the construction of the Interstate Highway System. PhD dissertation, University of Chicago.

Baumert, Kevin A., Timothy Herzog, and Jonathan Pershing. 2005. *Navigating the numbers: Greenhouse gases and international climate change agreements.* Washington, DC: World Resources Institute.

Baumgartner, Frank R., and Beth L. Leech. 1998. *Basic interests: The importance of groups in politics and in political science.* Princeton: Princeton University Press.

Baumgartner, Frank, and Bryan Jones. 1993. *Agendas and instability in American politics.* Chicago: University of Chicago Press.

Baxandall, Rosalyn, and Elizabeth Ewen. 2000. *Picture windows: How the suburbs happened.* New York: Basic Books.

Beatley, Timothy. 2000. *Green urbanism: Learning from the European cities.* Washington, DC: Island Press.

Beaubouef, Bruce A. 2007. *The strategic petroleum reserve: U.S. energy security and oil politics, 1975–2005.* College Station, TX: Texas A&M University Press.

Beauregard, Robert A. 2006. *When America became suburban.* Minneapolis: University of Minnesota Press.

Becker, Elizabeth. 2005, May 12. Trade deficit narrows to a 6-month low. *New York Times*, C7.

Becker, Helmut. 2006. *High noon in the automotive industry.* New York: Springer.

Bednar, Charles Sokol. 2003. *Transforming the dream: Ecologism and the shaping of an alternative American vision.* Albany: State University of New York Press.

Belcher, Wyatt Winton. 1947. *The economic rivalry between St. Louis and Chicago, 1850–1880.* New York: Columbia University Press.

Bento, Antonio, Maureen L. Cropper, Ahmed Mushfiq Mobarak, and Katja Vinha. 2005. The effects of urban spatial structure on travel demand in the United States. *The Review of Economics and Statistics* 87, no. 3: 466–78.

Berman, Edward H. 1983. *The ideology of philanthropy: The influence of the Carnegie, Ford, and Rockefeller Foundations on American foreign policy.* Albany: State University of New York Press.

Bernstein, Michael A. 1987. *The Great Depression: Delayed recovery and economic change in America, 1929–1939.* New York: Cambridge University Press.

Bhagwati, Jagdish N. 2004. *In defense of globalization.* New York: Oxford University Press.

Bill, James A. 1988. *The eagle and the lion: The tragedy of American-Iranian relations.* New Haven: Yale University Press.

Black, Brian. 2000. *Petrolia: The landscape of America's first oil boom.* Baltimore: Johns Hopkins University Press.

Blair, John M. 1976. *The control of oil.* New York: Pantheon.

Blas, Javier, James Boxell, and Kevin Morrison. 2005, May 4. Energy investment too small to meet growth in demand, warns watchdog. *Financial Times*, 1.

Blatt, Harvey. 2005. *America's environmental report card: Are we making the grade?* Cambridge: MIT Press.

Block, Fred. 1987. *Revising state theory: Essays in politics and postindustrialism.* Philadelphia: Temple University Press.

———. 1990. *Postindustrial possibilities: A critique of economic discourse.* Los Angeles: University of California Press.

Bloom, Nicholas. 2008. *Public housing that worked: New York in the twentieth century.* Philadelphia: University of Pennsylvania Press.

Bogart, William T. 2006. *Don't call it sprawl: Metropolitan structure in the twenty-first century.* Cambridge: Cambridge University Press.

Bohan, Caren. 2006, Nov. 28. Bush says U.S. to stay in Iraq till mission complete.Reuters.

Bonker, Don. 1988. *America's trade crisis: The making of the U.S. trade deficit.* Boston: Houghton Mifflin.

Borak, Donna 2006, Feb. 10. U.S. trade deficit reaches all-time high. United Press International (UPI).

Bosso, Christopher. 1987. *Pesticides and politics: The life cycle of a public issue.* Pittsburgh: University of Pittsburgh Press.

———. 2005. *Environment, Inc.: From grassroots to beltway.* Lawrence: University Press of Kansas.

Bottles, Scott. 1987. *Los Angeles and the automobile: The making of the modern city.* Los Angeles: University of California Press.

Boudette, Neal E., and Norihiko Shirouzu. 2008, May 20. Car makers' boom years now look like a bubble. *Wall Street Journal*, A1.

Bowles, Samuel, David M. Gordon, and Thomas E. Weisskopf. 1983. *Beyond the waste land: A Democratic alternative to economic decline.* Garden City, NY: Anchor Press/Doubleday.

Boyer, Robert and Daniel Drache. 1996. *States against markets: The limits of globalization.* New York: Routledge.

Bradford, Travis. 2006. *Solar revolution: The economic transformation of the global energy industry.* Cambridge: MIT Press.

Bradsher, Keith. 2002. *High and mighty: SUVs—The world's most dangerous vehicles and how they got that way.* New York: Public Affairs.

Braman, Sandra. 2006. *Change of state: Information, policy, and power.* Cambridge: MIT Press.

Braudel, Fernand. 1982/1984. *Civilization and capitalism, 15th–18th century.* Vols. 1–3. New York: Harper and Row.

Brenner, Robert. 2002. *The boom and the bubble: The U. S. in the world economy.* New York: Verso.

———. 2004, Jan./Feb. New boom or new bubble: The trajectory of the U.S. economy. *New Left Review* 25: 57–102.

Brienes, Marvin. 1975. The fight against smog in Los Angeles, 1943–1957. PhD Thesis, University of California, Davis.

———. 1976. Smog comes to Los Angeles. *Southern California Quarterly* 58, no. 4: 515–32.

Broder, John M. 2007, Dec. 19. House, 314–100, passes broad energy bill; Bush to sign it today. *New York Times*, A24.

Bromley, Simon. 1991. *American hegemony and world oil: The industry, the state system and the world economy.* University Park: Pennsylvania State University Press.

Bronson, Rachel. 2006. *Thicker than oil: America's uneasy partnership with Saudi Arabia.* New York: Oxford University Press.

Brown, Donald A. 2002. *American heat: Ethical problems with the United States' response to global warming.* Lanham, MD.: Rowman and Littlefield.

Brownell, Blaine. 1975. *The urban ethos in the South.* Baton Rouge: Louisiana State University Press.

Bruegmann, Robert. 2005. *Sprawl: A compact history.* Chicago: University of Chicago Press.

Bryner, Gary C. 1995. *Blue skies, green politics: The Clean Air Act of 1990 and its implementation,* 2nd ed. Washington, DC: Congressional Quarterly Press.

Buenger, Walter L., and Joseph A. Pratt. 1986. *But also good business: Texas commerce banks and the financing of Houston and Texas, 1886–1986.* College Station: Texas A&M University Press.

Bulkeley, Harriet, and Michele M. Betsill. 2003. *Cities and climate change: Urban sustainability and global environmental governance.* New York: Routledge.

Bullard, Robert D. 1990. *Dumping in Dixie.* Boulder: Westview.

———. 1997. Preface. In *Just transportation: Dismantling race and class barriers to mobility,* ed. Robert D. Bullard and Glenn S. Johnson. Stony Creek, CT: New Society Publishers.

———, ed. 2005. *The quest for environmental justice: Human rights and the politics of pollution.* San Francisco: Sierra Club Books.

———, ed. 2007. *Growing smarter: Achieving livable communities, environmental justice, and regional equity.* Cambridge: MIT Press.

Bullard, Robert D., and Glenn S. Johnson, eds. 1997. *Just transportation: Dismantling race and class barriers to mobility.* Stony Creek, CT: New Society Publishers.

Bullard, Robert D., Glenn S. Johnson, and Angel O. Torres, eds. 2000. *Sprawl city: Race, politics, and planning in Atlanta.* Washington, DC: Island Press.

Bullitt, William C., Under Secretary of the Navy. 1943, June. To the President (of the United States). In *A documentary history of the Petroleum Reserves Corporation, 1943–1944: Prepared for the use of Subcommittee on Multinational Corporations of the Committee on Foreign Relations, United States Senate, May 8, 1974.* Washington, DC: U.S. Government Printing Office: 3–6.

Bumiller, Elisabeth, and Carl Hulse. 2005, April 21. Bush concedes energy bill offers no help on gas prices. *New York Times,* A18.

Bunkley, Nick. 2008, Jan. 24. In global race, G.M. wins by a day of pickup sales. *New York Times,* C2.

———. 2008, Aug. 12. An S.U.V traffic jam. *New York Times,* C1.

Bupp, Irvin C., and Jean-Claude Derian. 1978. *The failed promise of nuclear power: The story of light water.* New York: Basic Books.

Burchell, Robert W., Anthony Downs, Barbara McCann, and Sahan Mukherji. 2005. *Sprawl costs: Economic impacts of unchecked development.* Washington, DC: Island Press.

Burkett, Paul. 1999. *Marx and nature: A red and green perspective.* New York: St. Martin's.

Burnham, John Cheynoweth. 1961. The gasoline tax and the automobile revolution. *Mississippi Valley Historical Review* 48, no. 3: 435–59.

Büthe, Tim. 2002. Taking temporality seriously: Modeling history and the use of narratives as evidence. *American Political Science Review* 96, no. 3: 481–93.

By-laws of the Petroleum Reserves Corporation, as amended, August 9, 1943. In *A documentary history of the Petroleum Reserves Corporation, 1943–1944: Prepared for the use of Subcommittee on Multinational Corporations of the Committee on Foreign Relations, United States Senate, May 8, 1974.* Washington, DC: U.S. Government Printing Office: 20–23.

Cahn, Matthew A. 1995. *Environmental deceptions: The tension between liberalism and environmental policymaking in the United States.* Albany: State University of New York Press.

Calder, Lendol. 1999. *Financing the American dream: A cultural history of consumer credit.* Princeton: Princeton University Press.

California Council for Environmental and Economic Balance (CCEEB). 2000. *Mission.* San Francisco: California Council for Environmental and Economic Balance.

Campbell, Kurt M., ed. 2008. *Climate cataclysm: The foreign policy and national security implications of climate change.* Washington, DC: Brookings.

Carpenter, Daniel P. 2001. *The forging of bureaucratic autonomy: Reputations, networks, and policy innovations in executive agencies, 1862–1928.* Princeton: Princeton University Press.

Carskadon, Thomas Reynolds, and George Henry Soule. 1957. *USA in new dimensions: The measure and promise of America's resources, a Twentieth Century Fund survey.* New York: Macmillan.

Carter, Neil. 2007. *The politics of the environment: Ideas, activism, policy,* 2nd ed. New York: Cambridge University Press.

Casner, Nicholas. 1999. Polluter versus polluter: The Pennsylvania Railroad and the manufacturing of pollution policies in the 1920s. *Journal of Policy History* 11, no. 2: 179–200.

Cass, Loren R. 2006. *The failures of American and European climate policy: International norms, domestic politics, and unachievable commitments.* Albany: State University of New York Press.

Castells, Manuel. 1996/1998. *The information age: Economy, society, and culture.* Vols. 1–3. Malden, MA: Blackwell.

Chalmers, Hugh. 1911. Relation of the automobile industry to the Good Roads Movement. In *Papers, addresses, and resolutions before the American Road Congress, Richmond, Virginia, November 20–23, 1911,* by the American Road Congress. Baltimore: Waverly Press.

Chang, Ha-Joon. 2008. *Bad Samaritans: The myth of free trade and the secret history of capitalism.* New York: Bloomsbury Press.

Cheape, Charles W. 1980. *Moving the masses: Urban public transit in New York, Boston, and Philadelphia, 1880–1912.* Cambridge: Harvard University Press.

Chichilnisky, Graciela, and Geoffrey Heal, eds. 2000. *Environmental markets: Equity and Efficiency.* New York: Columbia University Press.

Christoff, Peter. 1996. Ecological modernization, ecological modernities. *Environmental Politics* 5, no. 3: 476–500.

Clark, Brett, and Richard York. 2005. Carbon metabolism: Global capitalism, climate change, and the biospheric rift. *Theory and Society* 34 no. 4: 391–428.

Clawson, Dan, Alan Neustadtl, and Mark Weller. 1998. *Dollars and votes: How business campaign contributions subvert democracy.* Philadelphia: Temple University Press.

Cline, William R. 1992. *The economics of global warming.* Washington, DC: Institute for International Economics.

———. 2005. *The United States as a debtor nation.* Washington, DC: Institute for International Economics: Center for Global Development.

Coase, R. H. 1960. The problem of social cost. *Journal of Law and Economics* 3 (October): 1–44.

Cohen, Jean L. and Andrew Arato. 1992. *Civil society and political theory.* Cambridge: MIT Press.

Cohen, Lizabeth. 2003. Is there an urban history of consumption? *Journal of Urban History* 29, no. 2: 87–106.

Cohen, Michael P. 1988. *The history of the Sierra Club, 1892–1970.* San Francisco: Sierra Club Books.

Commission for Energy. 1956. *Europe's growing needs of energy: How can they be met?* Paris: Organization for European Economic Co-Operation.

Commons, John R. 1924. *Legal foundations of capitalism.* New York: Macmillan.

Connolly, William E. 2005. *Pluralism.* Durham: Duke University Press.

Conte, Christopher R. 2000. The boys of sprawl: Free-market think tanks opposed to smart growth. *Governing* 13, no. 8: 28–33.

Convery, Frank J., ed. 1998. *A guide to policies for energy conservation: The European experience.* Northampton, MA: Edward Elgar.

Conybeare, John A. C. 2004. *Merging traffic: The consolidation of the international automobile industry.* Lanham, MD: Rowman and Littlefield.

Crenson, Matthew A. 1971. *The un-politics of air pollution.* Baltimore: Johns Hopkins University Press.

Cronon, William. 1991. *Nature's metropolis: Chicago and the Great West.* New York: Norton.

Crump, Spencer. 1988. *Ride the big Red Cars: The Pacific Electric Story*, 7th ed. Glendale, CA: Trans-Anglo.

Curcio, Vincent. 2000. *Chrysler: The life and times of an automotive genius.* New York: Oxford University Press.

Cushman Jr., John H. 2002, July 2. California lawmakers vote to lower auto emissions. *New York Times*, A14.

Cyphers, Christopher J. 2002. The national civic federation and the making of new liberalism, 1900–1915. Westport, CT: Praeger.

Dahl, Robert A. 1956. *A preface to democratic theory.* Chicago: University of Chicago Press.

———. 1958. A critique of the ruling elite model. *American Political Science Review* 52, no. 2: 463–69.

———. 1959. Business and politics: A critical appraisal of political science. *American Political Science Review* 53, no. 1: 1–34.

———. 1961 [2005]. *Who governs?: Democracy and power in an American city.* New Haven: Yale University Press.

Dahl, Robert A., and Charles E. Lindblom. 1953. *Politics, economics, and welfare.* New Haven: Yale University Press.

———. 1976. Preface. In *Politics, economics, and welfare.* New Haven: Yale University Press.

Davis, David. 1993. *Energy politics.* New York: St. Martin's.

Davis, Devra. 2002. *When smoke ran like water: Tales of environmental deception and the battle against pollution.* New York: Basic Books.

Davis, Donald F. 1988. *Conspicuous production: Automobiles and elites in Detroit, 1899–1933.* Philadelphia: Temple University Press.

Davison, Aidan. 2001. *Technology and the contested meanings of sustainability.* Albany: State University of New York Press.

Dawson, Jane, and Robert Darst. 2006. Meeting the challenge of permanent nuclear waste disposal in an expanding Europe: Transparency, trust, and democracy. *Environmental Politics* 15, no. 4: 610–27.

Dawson, Michael. 2003. *The consumer trap: Big business marketing in American life.* Chicago: University of Illinois Press.

DeCicco, John, and Freda Fung, with Feng An. 2006. *Global warming on the road: The climate impact of America's automobiles.* Washington, DC: Environmental Defense.

Deffeyes, Kenneth S. 2001. *Hubbert's Peak: The impending world oil shortage.* Princeton: Princeton University Press.

———. 2005. *Beyond oil: The view from Hubbert's Peak.* New York: Hill and Wang.

DeGrove, John M. 2005. *Planning policy and politics: Smart growth and the states.* Cambridge, MA: Lincoln Land Institute.

DePalma, Anthony. 2005, Dec. 21. Seven states agree on a regional program to reduce emissions from power plants. *New York Times,* B3.

Desai, Uday, ed. 2002. *Environmental politics and policy in industrialized countries.* Cambridge: MIT Press.

Dessler, Andrew E., and Edward A. Parson. 2006. *The science and politics of global climate change: A guide to the debate.* Cambridge: Cambridge University Press.

Dewees, Donald N. 1970. The decline of the American street railways. *Traffic Regulation* 24: 563–81.

Dewey, Scott. 2000. *Don't breathe the air: Air pollution and U.S. environmental politics, 1945–1970.* College Station: Texas A&M University Press.

Dewhurst, Frederic, and the Twentieth Century Fund. 1955. *America's needs and resources: A new survey.* New York: Twentieth Century Fund.

Diaz, Henry F., and Richard J. Murnane, eds. 2008. *Climate extremes and society.* New York: Cambridge University Press.

Dilworth, Richardson. 2005. *The urban origins of suburban autonomy.* Cambridge: Harvard University Press.

Doherty, Brian. 2002. *Ideas and actions in the Green movement.* New York: Routledge.

Domhoff, G. William. 1967. *Who rules America?* Englewood Cliffs, NJ: Prentice-Hall.

———. 1970. *The higher circles: The governing class in America.* New York: Vintage.

———. 1974. *The Bohemian Grove and other retreats.* New York: Harper and Row.

———. 1978a. *The powers that be.* New York: Random House.

———. 1978b. *Who really rules: New Haven and community power reexamined.* Santa Monica: Goodyear.

———. 1990. *The power elite and the state.* New York: Aldine de Gruyter.

———. 1996. *State autonomy or class dominance?: Case studies on policy making in America.* New York: Aldine de Gruyter.

———. 2005. *Who rules America? Power, politics, and social change,* 5th ed. New York: McGraw-Hill.

Dowie, Mark. 1995. *Losing ground: American environmentalism at the close of the twentieth century.* Cambridge: MIT Press.

———. 2001. *American foundations: An investigative history.* Cambridge: MIT Press.

Dreier, Peter, John Mollenkopf, and Todd Swanstrom. 2001. *Place matters: Metropolitics for the twenty-first century.* Lawrence: University Press of Kansas.

Dryzek, John S. 1987. *Rational ecology: Environment and political economy.* New York: Blackwell.

———. 1996a. Political inclusion and the dynamics of democratization. *American Political Science Review* 90, no. 1: 475–87.

———. 1996b. *Democracy in capitalist times.* New York: Oxford University Press.

———. 2005. *The politics of the earth,* 2nd ed. New York: Oxford University Press.

———. 2006. *Deliberative global politics: Discourse and democracy in a divided world.* Cambridge: Polity Press.

Dryzek, John S., David Downs, Christian Hunold, and David Schlosberg, with Hans-Kristian Hernes. 2003. *Green states and social movements: Environmentalism in the United States, United Kingdom, Germany, and Norway.* New York: Oxford University Press.

Duany, Andres, Elizabeth Plater-Zyberk, and Jeff Speck. 2000. *Suburban nation: The rise of sprawl and the decline of the American dream.* New York: North Point Press.

Du Boff, Richard B. 1989. *Accumulation and power: An economic history of the United States.* Armonk, NY: M. E. Sharpe.

Duffield, John S. 2008. *Over a barrel: The costs of U.S. foreign oil dependence.* Stanford: Stanford University Press.

Duffy, Robert J. 2003. *The green agenda in American politics: New strategies for the twenty-first century.* Lawrence: University Press of Kansas.

Duménil, Gérard, and Dominique Lévy. 2004. *Capital resurgent: Roots of the neoliberal revolution.* Trans. Derek Jeffers. Cambridge: Harvard University Press.

Dunn, James. 1981. *Miles to go: European and American transportation policies.* Cambridge: MIT Press.

———. 1998. *Driving forces: The automobile, its enemies, and the politics of mobility.* Washington, DC: Brookings Institution Press.

Eakins, David. 1969. Business Planners and America's Postwar Expansion. In *Corporations and the cold war,* ed. David Horowitz. New York: Monthly Review Press.

———. 1972. Policy-planning for the Establishment. In *A new history of Leviathan*, ed. Ronald Radosh and Murray N. Rothberg. New York: E. P. Dutton.

Edelman, Murray. 1964. *The symbolic uses of politics*. Urbana: University of Illinois Press.

———. 1977. *Political language*. New York: Academic Press.

———. 1988. *Constructing the political spectacle*. Chicago: University of Chicago Press.

Eisinger, Peter K. 1988. *The rise of the entrepreneurial state: State and local economic development policy in the United States*. Madison: The University of Wisconsin Press.

Elkin, Stephen L. 1987. *City and regime in the American Republic*. Chicago: University of Chicago Press.

Elliott, John Huxtable. 2006. *Empires of the Atlantic world: Britain and Spain in America, 1492–1830*. New Haven: Yale University Press.

Ely, Richard T. 1914. *Property and contract in their relations to the distribution of wealth*. Vols. 1–2. New York: Macmillan.

Energy Advisory Commission. 1960. *Towards a new energy pattern in Europe*. Paris: Organization for European Economic Co-operation.

Energy efficiency fails to cut consumption—study. 2007, Nov. 27. Reuters.

Energy Information Administration (EIA). 1998. *Impacts of the Kyoto Protocol on US energy markets and economic activity*. Washington, DC: U.S. Department of Energy.

———. 2004. *Annual energy review 2003*. Washington, DC: U.S. Department of Energy.

———. 2007. *Annual energy review 2006*. Washington, DC: U.S. Department of Energy.

———. 2008. *Short-term energy outlook*. Washington, DC: U.S. Department of Energy.

Energy rhetoric and reality. 2007, Jan. 25. *New York Times*, A24.

*Environmental Performance Index*. 2006. New Haven: Yale Center for Environmental Law and Policy.

Erie, Steven P. 2004. *Globalizing L.A.: Trade, infrastructure, regional development*. Stanford: Stanford University Press.

———. 2006 *Beyond Chinatown: The Metropolitan Water District, growth, and the environment in Southern California*. Stanford: Stanford University Press.

Erlanger, Steven. 2008, Aug. 17. French plans for energy reaffirm nuclear path. *New York Times*, A6.

Evans, Peter B. 1997. The eclipse of the state? Reflections on stateness in an Era of globalization. *World Politics* 50, no. 1: 62–87.

Everly, John. 2005, July 3. Energy legislation could open "new markets." Dubuque, IA, *Telegraph Herald*, B4.

Ewing, Reid, Keith Bartholomew, Steve Winkelman, Jerry Walter, and Don Chen, with Barbara McCann, and David Goldberg. 2007. *Growing cooler: The evidence on urban development and climate change*. Chicago: Urban Land Institute.

Fackler, Martin. 2006, Aug. 5. Toyota's profit soars, helped by U.S. sales. *New York Times*, C4.

———. 2007, Jan. 6. Japan offers a lesson in using technology to reduce energy consumption. *New York Times*, C1.

———. 2008, May 9. Toyota expects decline in annual profit. *New York Times*, C3.

Farber, David. 2002. *Sloan rules: Alfred P. Sloan and the triumph of General Motors*. Chicago: University of Chicago Press.

Fearon, Peter. 1987. *War, prosperity, and depression: The U.S. Economy 1917–45*. Lawrence: University Press of Kansas.

Fein, Michael R. 2008. *Paving the way: New York road building and the American state, 1880–1956*. Lawrence: University of Kansas Press.

Ferrier, R. W. 1982. *The history of the British Petroleum Company*. Vol. 1. New York: Cambridge University Press.

Field, Alexander J. 2006. Technological change and U.S. productivity growth in the interwar years. *Journal of Economic History* 66, no. 1: 203–36.

Finegold, Kenneth, and Theda Skocpol. 1995. *State and party in America's New Deal*. Madison: University of Wisconsin Press.

Firebaugh, Glenn, and Brian Goesling. 2004. Accounting for the recent decline in global income inequality. *American Journal of Sociology* 110, no. 2: 283–312.

Fisher, Dana. 2004. *National governance and the global climate change regime*. Lanham, MD: Rowman and Littlefield.

Fisher, Peter S., and Alan H. Peters. 1998. *Industrial incentives: Competition among American states and cities*. Kalamazoo: W. E. Upjohn Institute.

Fishman, Robert. 1987. *Bourgeois utopias: The rise and fall of suburbia*. New York: Basic Books.

Fletcher, Martin, and Robin Pagnamenta. 2008, Feb. 1. Soaring oil prices and rising production fuel Iraq's economic revival. *The Times* (London), 2.

Flink, James. 1975. *The car culture*. Cambridge: MIT Press.

———. 1990. *The automobile age*. Cambridge: MIT Press.

Flint, Anthony. 2006. *This land: The battle over sprawl and the future of America*. Baltimore: Johns Hopkins University Press.

Fogelson, Robert M. 1967. *The fragmented metropolis, Los Angeles, 1850–1930*. Cambridge: Harvard University Press.

———. 2001. *Downtown: Its rise and fall, 1880–1950*. New Haven: Yale University Press.

———. 2005. *Bourgeois nightmares: Suburbia, 1870–1930*. New Haven: Yale University Press.

Foley, Duncan K. 2003. *Unholy trinity: Labor, capital, and land in the new economy*. New York: Routledge.

Ford, Royal. 2004, Feb. 15. Good, bad, and ugly of fuel efficiency. *Boston Globe*, J5.

Foreign Operations Committee, of the Petroleum Administration for War. 1943, November 5. A foreign oil policy for the United States. In *A documentary history of the Petroleum Reserves Corporation, 1943–1944: Prepared for the use of Subcommittee on Multinational Corporations of the Committee on Foreign Relations, United States Senate, May 8, 1974*. Washington, DC: U.S. Government Printing Office, 60–68.

Foss, Phillip O. 1960. *Politics and grass*. Seattle: University of Washington Press.

Foster, Mark S. 1975. The Model-T, the hard sell, and Los Angeles's urban growth: The decentralization of Los Angeles during the 1920s. *Pacific Historical Review* 44 (Nov.): 459–84.

———. 1981. *From streetcar to superhighway: American city planners and urban transportation, 1900–1940*. Philadelphia: Temple University Press.

Franks, Kenny A., and Paul F. Lambert. 1982. *Early Louisiana and Arkansas oil*. College Station: Texas A&M University Press.

French, Michael. 1997. *U.S. economic history since 1945*. Manchester: Manchester University Press.

Friedman, Thomas L. 2005. *The World is flat: A brief history of the twenty-first century*. New York: Farrar, Straus and Giroux.

Frumkin, Howard, Lawrence Frank, and Richard Jackson. 2004. *Urban sprawl and public health: Designing, planning, and building for healthy communities*. Washington, DC: Island Press.

Frumkin, Norman. 2004. *Tracking America's economy*, 4th ed. Armonk, NY: M. E. Sharpe.

Gallagher, Kelly Sims. 2006. *China shifts gears: Automakers, oil, pollution, and development*. Cambridge: MIT Press.

Gallagher, Mary Elizabeth. 2005. *Contagious capitalism: Globalization and the politics of labor in China*. Princeton: Princeton University Press.

Game, Kingsley. 1979. Controlling air pollution: Why some states try harder. *Policy Studies Journal* 7: 728–38.

Garofoli, Joe. 2005, April 23. New life through "death"—Authors shake up environmentalism with essay on movement's fatal flaws. *San Francisco Chronicle*, p. B1.

Gautier, Catherine. 2008. *Oil, water, and climate: An introduction*. New York: Cambridge University Press.

Gautier, Catherine, and Jean-Louis Fellous, eds. 2008. *Facing climate change together*. New York: Cambridge University Press.

Gelpi, Rosa-Maria, and François Julien-Labruyère. 2000. *The history of consumer credit: Doctrines and practices*. New York: St. Martin's.

Gertner, Jon. 2006, July 16. Atomic balm? *New York Times Magazine*, sec. 6, 36.

Gillham, Oliver. 2002. *The limitless city*. Washington, DC: Island Press.

Gilpin, Robert. 1987. *The political economy of international relations*. Princeton: Princeton University Press.

Glyn, Andrew. 2006. *Capitalism unleashed: Finance globalization and welfare*. New York: Oxford University Press.

Gonzalez, George A. 1998. The conservation policy network, 1890–1910: The development and implementation of "practical" forestry. *Polity*: 31, no. 2: 269–99.

———. 1999, June. Review of *Pluralism-by-the-rules*, by Edward P. Weber. *American Political Science Review* 93, no. 2: 461–62.

———. 2000. Review of *Voices and echoes for the environment*, by Ronald Shaiko, and *Eco-wars*, by Ronald Libby. *American Political Science Review* 94, no. 4: 950–51.

————. 2001a. *Corporate power and the environment: The political economy of U.S. environmental policy.* Lanham, MD: Rowman and Littlefield.

————. 2001b. Ideas and state capacity, or business dominance? A historical analysis of grazing on the public grasslands. *Studies in American Political Development* 15 (Fall): 234–44.

————. 2002/03. Urban growth and the politics of air pollution: The establishment of California's automobile emission standards. *Polity* 35, no. 2: 213–36.

————. 2005a. *The politics of air pollution: Urban growth, ecological modernization, and symbolic inclusion.* Albany: State University of New York Press.

————. 2005b. The Comprehensive Everglades Restoration Plan: Economic or environmental sustainability? *Polity* 37, no. 4: 466–90.

Goodman, Peter S. 2007, Nov. 25. The U.S. economy: Trying to guess what happens next. *New York Times*, sec. 4, 1.

————. 2008, Feb. 5. Economy fitful, Americans start to pay as they go. *New York Times*, A1.

————. 2008, June 25. Fuel prices shift math for life in far suburbs. *New York Times*, A18.

————. 2008, Aug. 24. U.S. and global economies slipping in unison. *New York Times*, A1.

Goodman, Peter S., and Nell Henderson. 2007, Feb. 14. Oil prices, imported goods push trade gap to record. *Washington Post*, A1.

Goodstein, David. 2004. *Out of gas: The end of the age of oil.* New York: Norton.

Gordon, Bernard K. 2001. *America's trade follies: Turning economic leadership into strategic weakness.* New York: Routledge.

Gordon, Colin. 1994. *New Deals: Business, labor, and politics in America, 1920–1935.* New York: Cambridge University Press.

Gorz, Andre. 1994. *Capitalism, socialism, ecology.* Boulder: Westview.

Gotham, Kevin F. 2000. Racialization and the state: The Housing Act of 1934 and the creation of the Federal Housing Administration. *Sociological Perspectives* 43, no. 2: 291–317.

————. 2002. *Race, real estate, and uneven development.* Albany: State University of New York Press.

————. 2006. The secondary circuit of capital reconsidered: Globalization and the U.S. real estate sector. *American Journal of Sociology* 112, no. 1: 231–75.

Gough, Ian. 2000. *Global capital, human needs, and social policies.* New York: St. Martin's.

Graham, Otis L. 1976. *Toward a planned society: From Roosevelt to Nixon.* New York: Oxford University Press.

Grant, Wyn. 1996. *Autos, smog, and pollution control.* Brookfield, VT: Edward Elgar.

Greenberg, Edward S., and Benjamin I. Page. 2005. *The struggle for democracy,* 7th ed. New York: Pearson Longman.

Greenspan defends homeowner debt levels. 2004, Oct. 20. *Chattanooga Times Free Press*, C2.

Greenwatch. 2007. *The climate change performance index:2008.* Berlin: Greenwatch.

Greider, William. 1997. *One world, ready or not: The manic logic of global capitalism*. New York: Simon and Schuster.

Gries, John M., and James Ford, eds. 1932. *The president's conference on home builders and home ownership: Home finance and taxation*. Washington, DC: National Capital Press.

Grossman, Gene M., and Elhanan Helpman. 2001. *Special interest politics*. Cambridge: MIT Press.

Guadalupe, Maria, and Moog Rodrigues. 2004. *Global environmentalism and local politics*. Albany: State University of New York Press.

Guber, Deborah Lynn. 2003. *The grassroots of a green revolution: Polling America on the environment*. Cambridge: MIT Press.

Gutfreund, Owen D. 2004. *Twentieth-century sprawl: Highways and the reshaping of the American landscape*. New York: Oxford University Press.

Hajer, Maarten A. 1995. *The politics of environmental discourse*. New York: Oxford University Press.

Hakim, Danny. 2003, April 25. California regulators modify auto emissions mandate. *New York Times*, A24.

———. 2003, Aug. 12. Automakers drop suits on air rules. *New York Times*, A1.

———. 2005, May 21. A love affair with S.U.V.'s begins to cool. *New York Times*, A1.

———. 2005, Aug. 4. Toyota develops hybrids with an eye on the future. *New York Times*, C3.

Hansen, Susan B. 2006. *Globalization and the politics of pay: Policy choices in the American states*. Washington, DC: Georgetown University Press.

Hardt, Michael, and Antonio Negri. 2000. *Empire*. Cambridge: Harvard University Press.

Harrington, Winston, and Virginia McConnell. 2003. *Resources for the Future report: Motor vehicles and the environment*. Washington, DC: Resources for the Future.

Harvey, David. 1985. *The urbanization of capital: Studies in the history and theory of capitalist urbanization*. Baltimore: Johns Hopkins University Press.

———. 2005. *The new imperialism*. Oxford: Oxford University Press.

Harvey, Mark. 2005. *Wilderness forever: Howard Zahniser and the path to the Wilderness Act*. Seattle: University of Washington Press.

Hasegawa, Yozo. 2008. *Clean car wars: How Honda and Toyota are winning the battle of the eco-friendly autos*, trans. Tony Kimm. Singapore: John Wiley and Sons.

Hatch, Michael T. 1986. *Politics and nuclear power: Energy policy in Western Europe*. Lexington: University Press of Kentucky.

———. 2005. *Environmental policymaking: Assessing the use of alternative policy instruments*. Albany: State University of New York Press.

Haugland, Torleif, Helge Ole Bergensen, and Kjell Roland. 1998. *Energy structures and environmental futures*. New York: Oxford University Press.

Hay, Colin, Michael Lister, and David Marsh, eds. 2006. *The state: Theories and issues*. New York: Palgrave Macmillan.

Hayden, Dolores. 2003. *Building suburbia: Green fields and urban growth, 1820–2000*. New York: Pantheon.

Hays, Samuel. 1964. The politics of reform in municipal government in the Progressive Era. *Pacific Northwest Quarterly* 55, no. 4: 157–69.

Hayward, Clarissa Rile. 2000. *De-facing power*. New York: Cambridge University Press.

Hecht, Gabrielle. 1998. *The radiance of France: Nuclear power and national identity after World War II*. Cambridge: MIT Press.

Heclo, Hugh. 1978. Issue networks and the executive establishment. In *The new American political system*, ed. Anthony King. Washington, DC: American Enterprise Institute for Public Policy Research.

Heilprin, John. 2007, Feb. 2. White House rejects mandatory $CO_2$ caps. Associated Press.

Heinberg, Richard. 2005. *The party's over: Oil, war, and the fate of industrial societies*, 2$^{nd}$ ed. Gabriola Island, CAN: New Society Publishers.

Heinz, John P., Edward O. Laumann, Robert L. Nelson, and Robert H. Salisbury. 1993. *The hollow core: Private interests in national policymaking*. Cambridge: Harvard University Press.

Henthorn, Cynthia Lee. 2006. *From submarines to suburbs: Selling a better America, 1939–1959*. Columbus: Ohio State University Press.

Hernandez, Ramona. 2002. *The mobility of labor under advanced capitalism: Dominican migration to the United States*. New York: Columbia University Press.

Herring, Horace, and Steve Sorrell. 2009. *Energy efficiency and sustainable consumption: The rebound effect*. New York: Palgrave Macmillan.

Hess, David J. 2007. *Alternative pathways in science and industry: Activism, innovation, and the environment in an era of globalization*. Cambridge: MIT Press.

Higgins-Evenson, R. Rudy. 2003. *The price of progress: Public services, taxation, and the American corporate state, 1877 to 1929*. Baltimore: Johns Hopkins University Press.

Hirt, Paul W. 1994. *A conspiracy of optimism: Management of the national forests since World War Two*. Lincoln: University of Nebraska Press.

Hise, Greg. 1997. *Magnetic Los Angeles: Planning the twentieth-century metropolis*. Baltimore: Johns Hopkins University Press.

———. 2001. "Nature's workshop" Industry and urban expansion in Southern California, 1900–1950. *Journal of Historical Geography* 27, no. 1: 74–92.

Hohenstein, Kurt. 2008. *Coining corruption: The making of the American campaign finance system*. DeKalb: Northern Illinois University Press.

Holter, Darryl. 1992. *The battle for coal: Miners and the politics of nationalization in France, 1940–1950*. DeKalb: Northern Illinois University Press.

Hornborg, Alf. 2001. *The power of the machine: Global inequalities of economy, technology, and environment*. Walnut Creek, CA: Altamira.

Hornstein, Jeffrey M. 2005. *A nation of realtors: A cultural history of the twentieth-century American middle class*. Durham: Duke University Press.

Houghton, John T. 2004. *Global warming: The complete briefing*, 3$^{rd}$ ed. New York: Cambridge University Press.

Hovi, Jon, Tora Skodvin, and Steinar Andresen. 2003. The persistence of the Kyoto Protocol: Why other Annex I countries move on without the United States. *Global Environmental Politics* 3, no. 4: 1–22.

Hoyos, Carola, and Javier Bias. 2008, Oct. 29. World will struggle to meet oil demand. *Financial Times*, 1.

Hoyt, Homer. 1933. *One hundred years of land values in Chicago: The relationship of the growth of Chicago to the rise in its land values, 1830–1933.* Chicago: University of Chicago Press.

Hulse, Carl. 2005, June 17. Senate makes environment the focus of energy bill. *New York Times*, A16.

———. 2007, June 23. Vote on mileage reveals new configuration in the Senate. *New York Times*, A11.

Hunt, Michael H. 2007. *The American ascendancy: How the United States gained and wielded global dominance.* Chapel Hill: University of North Carolina Press.

Hyman, Sidney. 1976. *Marringer S. Eccles: Private entrepreneur and public servant.* Stanford: Stanford University Graduate School of Business.

Ikenberry, G. John. 1988. *Reasons of state: Oil politics and the capacities of American government.* Ithaca: Cornell University Press.

International Chamber of Commerce (ICC). 2003, December 12. Press release: Business backs technology solutions for climate change. Paris: International Chamber of Commerce.

International Chamber of Commerce (ICC) Commission on Environment and Energy. 2002. *Energy for sustainable development: Business recommendations and roles* Paris: International Chamber of Commerce.

———. 2007. *Business perspectives on a long-term international framework to address global climate change.* Paris: International Chamber of Commerce.

———. 2007, May. *Energy security: A worldwide business perspective.* Paris: International Chamber of Commerce.

International Energy Agency. 1997. *Indicators of energy use and efficiency: Understanding the link between energy and human activity.* Paris: International Energy Agency.

———. 2007. $CO_2$ *Emissions from fuel combustion: 1971–2005.* Paris: International Energy Agency.

———. 2007, July 9. *Medium-term oil market report.* Paris: International Energy Agency.

Iraq oil output lowest since invasion. 2006, April 28. Associated Press.

Isaac, Jeffrey. 1993. Civil society and the spirit of revolt. *Dissent* 40 (Summer): 356–61.

———. 2003. *The poverty of progressivism: The future of American democracy in a time of liberal decline.* Lanham, MD.: Rowman and Littlefield.

Isser, Steve. 1996. *The economics and politics of the United States oil industry, 1920–1990: Profits, populism, and petroleum.* New York: Routledge.

Jackson, Kenneth T. 1985. *Crabgrass frontier: The suburbanization of the United States.* New York: Oxford University Press.

Jacoby, Neil H. 1974. *Multinational oil: A study in industrial dynamics.* New York: Macmillan.

Jaher, Frederic Cople. 1982. *The urban establishment: Upper strata in Boston, New York, Charleston, Chicago, and Los Angeles.* Urbana: University Press of Illinois.

Jakle, John A., and Keith A. Sculle. 2008. *Motoring: The highway experience in America.* Athens: University of Georgia Press.

Jasper, James M. 1990. *Nuclear politics: Energy and the state in the United States, Sweden, and France.* Princeton: Princeton University Press.

Johnson, Elizabeth A., and Michael W. Klemens, eds. 2005. *Nature in fragments: The legacy of sprawl.* New York: Columbia University Press.

Jonas, Andrew E. G., and David Wilson, eds. 1999. *The urban growth machine: Critical perspectives two decades later.* Albany: State University of New York Press.

Jones, Bryan D., and Frank Baumgartner. 2005. *The politics of attention: How government prioritizes problems.* Chicago: University of Chicago Press.

Jones, Charles O. 1975. *Clean air.* Pittsburgh: University of Pittsburgh Press.

Jones, Holway R. 1965. *John Muir and the Sierra Club: The battle for Yosemite.* San Francisco: Sierra Club.

Jones, Joseph. 1984. *The politics of transport in twentieth-century France.* Montreal: McGill-Queen's University Press.

Juhasz, Antonia. 2007, March 13. Whose oil is it, anyway? *New York Times,* 19.

Kahn, Matthew E. 2006. *Green cities: Urban growth and the environment.* Washington, DC: Brookings.

Kamieniecki, Sheldon. 2006. *Corporate America and environmental policy: How often does business get its way?* Stanford: Stanford University Press.

Kamieniecki, Sheldon, and Michael Farrell. 1991. Intergovernmental relations and clean-air policy in Southern California. *Publius* 21, no. 3: 143–54.

Kamieniecki, Sheldon, David Shafie, and Julie Silvers. 1999. Forming partnerships in environmental policy. *American Behavioral Scientist* 43, no. 1: 107–23.

Kanter, James. 2007, July 10. Rise in world oil use and a possible shortage of supplies are seen in the next 5 years. *New York Times,* C4.

Karen, Mattias. 2005, June 7. Report: Military spending tops $1T mark. Associated Press.

Katzenstein, Peter J. 2005. *A world of regions: Asia and Europe in the American imperium.* Ithaca: Cornell University Press.

Kay, Jane Holtz. 1998. *Asphalt nation: How the automobile took over America and how we can take it back.* Berkeley: University of California Press.

Keating, Ann Durkin. 1988. *Building Chicago: Suburban developers and the creation of a divided metropolis.* Columbus: Ohio State University Press.

Keck, Margaret E., and Kathryn Sikkink. 1998. *Activists beyond borders: Advocacy networks in international politics.* Ithaca: Cornell University Press.

Keeler, Andrew G. 2007. State greenhouse gas reduction policies: A move in the right direction? *Policy Sciences* 40, no. 4: 353–65.

Kenworthy, Jeffrey R., and Felix B. Laube, with Peter Newman, Paul Barter, Tamim Raad, Chamlong Poboon, and Benedicto Guia Jr. 1999. *An international sourcebook of automobile dependence in cities 1960–1990.* Boulder: University Press of Colorado.

Klein, Maury. 2007. *The genesis of industrial America, 1870–1920.* New York: Cambridge University Press.

Klyza, Christopher. 1996. *Who controls the public lands?: Mining, forestry, and grazing policies, 1870–1990*. Chapel Hill: The University of North Carolina Press.

Knox, Paul L. *Metroburbia, USA*. Piscataway, NJ: Rutgers University Press.

Kohn, Margaret. 2003. *Radical space: Building the house of the people*. Ithaca: Cornell University Press.

Kolko, Gabriel. 1977 (1963). *The triumph of conservatism: A reinterpretation of American history, 1900–1916*. New York: Free Press.

Kong, Tat Yan. 2006. Globalization and the labour market. *British Journal of Political Science* 36, no. 2: 359–83.

Kozlowski, Paul J., and James K. Weekly. 1990. Explaining interstate variations in foreign direct investment in the United States. *Regional Science Perspectives* 20, no. 2: 3–25.

Kraft, Michael E. 1993. Air pollution in the West: Testing the limits of public support with Southern California's clean air policy. In *Environmental politics and policy in the West*, ed. Zachary Smith. Dubuque: Kendall/Hunt.

———. 1994. Environmental gridlock: Searching for consensus in Congress. In *Environmental policy in the 1990s*, 2nd ed., ed. N. J. Vig and M. E. Kraft. Washington, DC: Congressional Quarterly Press.

Kraft, Michael E., and Sheldon Kamieniecki, eds. 2007. *Business and environmental policy: Corporate interests in the American political system*. Cambridge: MIT Press.

Kramer, Andrew E. 2005, Dec. 28. In Russia, pollution is good for business. *New York Times*, C1.

Krasner, Stephen D. 1978. *Defending the national interest: Raw materials investments and U.S. Foreign Policy*. Princeton: Princeton University Press.

Krauss, Clifford. 2007, Jan. 23. U.S. lab a sign of America's fickle affair with renewable energy. *The International Herald Tribune*, sec. Finance, 9.

———. 2007, Nov. 2. Tapping a trickle in West Texas. *New York Times*, C1.

———. 2007, Dec. 18. As ethanol takes its first steps, Congress proposes a giant leap. *New York Times*, C1.

———. 2008, Oct. 14. Commodity prices tumble. *New York Times*, B1.

———. 2008, Oct. 21. Alternative energy suddenly faces headwinds. *New York Times*, B1.

Krier, James E., and Edmund Ursin 1977. *Pollution and policy: A case essay on California and federal experience with motor vehicle air pollution*. Los Angeles: University of California Press.

Kruse, Kevin M., and Thomas J. Sugrue, eds. 2006. *The new suburban history*. Chicago: University of Chicago Press.

Kütting, Gabriela. 2004. *Globalization and the environment: Greening global political economy*. Albany: State University of New York Press.

Laird, Frank N. 2001. *Solar energy, technology policy, and institutional values*. New York: Cambridge University Press.

Lamare, James W. 1993. *California politics*. New York: West.

———. 2000. *Texas politics: Economics, power, and policy*, 7th ed. Belmont: Wadsworth.

Lane, Julia, Dennis Clennon, and James McCabe. 1989. Measures of local business climate: Alternative approaches. *Regional Science Perspectives* 19, no. 1: 89–100.

Lanne, Markku, and Matti Liski. 2004. Trends and breaks in per-capita carbon dioxide emissions, 1870–2028. *Energy Journal* 25, no. 4: 41–65.

Lassiter, Matthew D. 2005. *The silent majority: Suburban politics in the Sunbelt South*. Princeton: Princeton University Press.

Layne, Christopher. 2006. *The peace of illusions: American grand strategy from 1940 to the present*. Ithaca: Cornell University Press.

Layzer, Judith A. 2007. Deep freeze: How business has shaped the global warming debate in Congress. In *Business and environmental policy*, ed. Michael E. Kraft and Sheldon Kamieniecki. Cambridge: MIT Press, 93–126.

Leahy, Stephen. 2007, March 21. Biofuels boom spurring deforestation. *Inter Press Service*.

Leggett, Jeremy K. 2005. *Half gone: Oil, gas, hot air, and the global energy crisis*. London: Portobello.

Levine, Jonathan. 2006. *Zoned out: Regulation, markets, and choices in transportation and metropolitan land-use*. Washington, DC: Resources for the Future.

Levy, David L., and Daniel Egan. 2003. A neo-Gramscian approach to corporate political strategy: Conflict and accommodation in the climate change negotiations. *Journal of Management Studies* 40, no. 4: 803–29.

Light, Ivan. 2006. *Deflecting immigration: How Los Angeles tamed globalization*. New York: Sage.

Lindblom, Charles E. 1977. *Politics and markets: The world's political-economic systems*. New York: Basic Books.

———. 1982. The market as prison. *Journal of Politics* 44, no. 2: 324–36.

———. 1983. Comment on Manley. *American Political Science Review* 77, no. 2: 384–86.

———. 1988. *Democracy and market system*. Oslo: Norwegian University Press.

Lisowski, Michael. 2002. Playing the two-level game: US president Bush's decision to repudiate the Kyoto Protocol. *Environmental Politics* 11, no. 4: 101–19.

Liu, Jianguo, Gretchen C. Daily, Paul R. Ehrlich, and Gary W. Luck. 2003, January 30. Effects of household dynamics on resource consumption and biodiversity. *Nature* 421: 530–33.

Logan, John R., and Harvey L. Molotch. 1987. *Urban fortunes: The political economy of place*. Berkeley: University of California Press.

Logan, Michael. 1995. *Fighting sprawl and city hall: Resistance to urban growth in the Southwest*. Tucson: University of Arizona Press.

Lomborg, Bjorn. 2001. *The skeptical environmentalist: Measuring the real state of the world*. New York: Cambridge University Press.

———. 2007. *Cool it: The skeptical environmentalist's guide to global warming*. New York: Knopf.

Lopez, Russ, and H. Patricia Hynes. 2003. Sprawl in the 1990s: Measurement, distribution, and trends. *Urban Affairs Review* 38, no. 3: 325–55.

Lotchin, Roger W. 1992. *Fortress California, 1910–1960*. New York: Oxford University Press.

Louter, David. 2006. *Windshield wilderness: Cars, roads, and nature in Washington's parks*. Seattle: University of Washington Press.

Lowery, David, and Virginia Gray. 2004. Review essay: A neopluralist perspective on research on organized interests. *Political Research Quarterly* 57, no. 1: 163–75.

Lowi, Theodore J. 1979. *The end of liberalism: The Second Republic of the United States*. New York: Norton.

Lowry, William R. 1992. *The dimensions of federalism: State governments and pollution control policies*. Durham: Duke University Press.

———. 1998. *Preserving public lands for the future: The politics of intergenerational goods*. Washington, DC: Georgetown University Press.

Lucas, Nigel. 1985. *Western European energy policies: A comparative study of the influence of institutional structures on technical change*. Oxford: Clarendon.

Luger, Stan. 2000. *Corporate power, American democracy, and the automobile industry*. New York: Cambridge University Press.

———. 2005. Review of *Sloan rules: Alfred P. Sloan and the triumph of General Motors*. *American Historical Review* 110, no. 1: 174–75.

Lyons, William M., Scott Peterson, and Kimberly Noerager. 2003. *Greenhouse gas reduction through state and local transportation planning*. Washington, DC: Department of Transportation.

MacKellar, F. Landis, Wolfgang Lutz, Christopher Prinz, and Anne Goujon. 1995. Population, households, and $CO_2$ emissions. *Population and Development Review* 21, no. 4: 849–55.

Mackin, Anne. 2006. *Americans and their land: The house built on abundance*. Ann Arbor: University of Michigan Press.

MacLachlan, Colin M. 2006. *Argentina: What went wrong*. London: Praeger.

Manley, John F. 1983. Neo-pluralism: A class analysis of Pluralism I and Pluralism II. *American Political Science Review* 77, no. 2: 368–83.

Marchand, B. 1986. *The emergence of Los Angles: Population and housing in the city of dreams, 1940–1970*. London: Pion.

Markusen, Ann. 1985. *Profit cycles, oligopoly, and regional development*. Cambridge: MIT Press.

Marsh, Bill. 2006, Dec. 24. What surrounds the Iraqi tinderbox. *New York Times*, sec.4, 10.

Marzotto, Toni, Vicky Moshier Burnor, and Gordon Scott Bonham. 2000. *The evolution of public policy: Cars and the environment*. Boulder: Lynne Rienner.

Maull, Hanns. 1980. *Europe and world energy*. London: Butterworths.

Maynard, Micheline. 2007, July 4. Toyota hybrid makes a statement, and that sells. *New York Times*, A1.

McConnell, Grant. 1966. *Private power and American democracy*. New York: Knopf.

McCright, Aaron M. and Riley E. Dunlap. 2000. Challenging global warming: An analysis of the conservative movement's counter-claims. *Social Problems* 47, no. 4: 499–522.

McDonald, Stephen L. 1971. *Petroleum conservation in the United States: An economic analysis*. Baltimore: Johns Hopkins University Press.

McFarland, Andrew S. 2004. *Neopluralism: The evolution of political process theory*. Lawrence: University Press of Kansas.

———. 2007. Neopluralism. *Annual Review of Political Science* 10, no 1: 45–66.

McGrath, Patrick J. 2002. *Scientists, business, and the state, 1890–1960*. Chapel Hill: University of North Carolina Press.

McKay, John P. 1976. *Tramways and trolleys: The rise of urban mass transit in Europe*. Princeton: Princeton University Press.

———. 1988. Comparative perspectives on transit in Europe and the United States, 1850–1914. In *Technology and the rise of the networked city in Europe and America*, ed. Joel A. Tarr and Gabriel Dupuy. Philadelphia: Temple University Press.

McShane, Clay. 1974. *Technology and reform: Street railways and the growth of Milwaukee, 1887–1900*. Madison: State Historical Society of Wisconsin.

———. 1994. *Down the asphalt path: The automobile and the American city*. New York: Columbia University Press.

Milbrath, Lester W. 1989. *Envisioning a sustainable society: Learning our way out*. Albany: State University of New York Press.

———. 1995. Psychological, cultural, and informational barriers to sustainability. *Journal of Social Issues* 51, no.4: 101–20.

———. 1996. *Learning to think environmentally*. Albany: State University of New York Press.

Miliband, Ralph. 1969. *The state in capitalist society*. New York: Basic Books.

Military tells Bush of troop strains. 2008, March 26. Associated Press.

Miller, Arthur Selwyn. 1976. *The modern corporate state: Private governments and the American Constitution*. Westport, CT: Greenwood.

Miller, Edward. 1973. Some implications of land ownership patterns for petroleum policy. *Land Economics* 49, no. 4: 414–23.

Miller, Roger. 1991. Selling Mrs. Consumer: Advertising and the creation of suburban socio-spatial relations, 1910–1930. *Antipode* 23, no. 3: 263–306.

Mills, C. Wright. 1956. *The power elite*. New York: Oxford University Press.

Mintz, Beth, and Michael Schwartz. 1985. *The power structure of American business*. Chicago: University of Chicago Press.

Mitchell, Timothy. 1991. The limits of the state: Beyond statist approaches and their critics. *American Political Science Review* 85, no. 1: 77–96.

Moehring, Eugene P. 2004. *Urbanism and empire in the Far West, 1840–1890*. Reno: University of Nevada Press.

Mol, Arthur P. J. 2001. *Globalization and environmental reform: The ecological modernization of the global economy*. Cambridge: MIT Press.

———. 2002. Ecological modernization and the global economy. *Global Environmental Politics* 2, no. 2: 92–115.

Mollenkopf, John C. 1983. *The contested city*. Princeton: Princeton University Press.

Molotch, Harvey. 1976. The city as a growth machine: Towards a political economy of place. *American Journal of Sociology* 82, no. 2: 309–22.

———. 1979. Capital and neighborhood in the United States. *Urban Affairs Quarterly* 14, no. 3: 289–312.

Monastersky, Richard. 2003, October 10. Running on fumes: University research into hydrogen-powered cars accelerates, but the technology faces many roadblocks. *Chronicle of Higher Education* 50, no. 7: A14.

Moore, Jason W. 2003. The modern world-system as environmental history? Ecology and the rise of capitalism. *Theory and Society* 32, no. 3: 307–77.

Moore, Matt. 2004, June 9. Global military spending soars. Associated Press.

Moroney, John R. 2008. *Power struggle: World energy in the twenty-first century*. Westport, CT: Praeger.

Motavalli, Jim. 2006, May 14. Solution or distraction? An ethanol reality check. *New York Times*, sec. 12, 2.

Mouawad, Jad. 2005, April 5. Chevron Texaco offers $16.8 billion for Unocal. *New York Times*, C1.

Mouawad, Jad, and Heather Timmons. 2006, April 29. Trading frenzy adds to jump in price of oil. *New York Times*, A1.

Mufson, Steven. 2008, Jan. 31. Plan for carbon storage dropped; Energy Dept. scraps FutureGen alliance. *Washington Post*, A7.

Muller, Peter. 1981. *Contemporary suburban America*. Englewood Cliffs, NJ: Prentice-Hall.

National Oil Policy Committee of the Petroleum Industry War Council. 1944, Feb. 28. A national oil policy for the United States. In *A documentary history of the Petroleum Reserves Corporation, 1943–1944: Prepared for the use of Subcommittee on Multinational Corporations of the Committee on Foreign Relations, United States Senate, May 8, 1974*. Washington, DC: U.S. Government Printing Office, 71–80.

Natural Resources Defense Council (NRDC). 2002, July 22. Press release: California Gov. Gray Davis signs landmark $CO_2$ pollution measure. Washington, DC: Natural Resources Defense Council.

———. 2005, June 9. Press release: Energy bill: Haste makes a wasted opportunity. Washington, DC: Natural Resources Defense Council.

Nau, Henry. 1974. *National politics and international technology: Nuclear reactor development in Western Europe*. Baltimore: Johns Hopkins University Press.

Nelkin, Dorothy, and Michael Pollak. 1981. *The atom besieged: Antinuclear movements in France and Germany*. Cambridge: MIT Press.

Nersesian, Roy L. 2007. *Energy for the 21st century*. Armonk, NY: M. E. Sharpe.

Neumayer, Eric. 2003. *Weak versus strong sustainability: Exploring the limits of two opposing paradigms*, 2nd ed. Northampton, MA: Edward Elgar.

Newman, Peter, and Jeffrey Kenworthy. 1999. *Sustainability and cities: Overcoming automobile dependence*. Washington, DC: Island Press.

Nexon, Daniel H., and Thomas Wright. 2007. What's at stake in the American Empire debate. *American Political Science Review* 101, no. 2: 253–71.

Nijkamp, Peter. 1994. *Sustainable cities in Europe: A comparative analysis of urban energy-environmental policies*. London: Earthscan.

Nivola, Pietro S. 1999. *Laws of the landscape: How policies shape cities in Europe and America*. Washington, DC: Brookings.

Nivola, Pietro S., and Robert W. Crandall. 1995. *The extra mile: Rethinking energy policy for automobile transportation*. Washington, DC: Brookings.

Noble, David F. 1977. *America by design.* New York: Oxford University Press.

Nordhaus, Ted, and Michael Shellenberger. 2007. *Break through. From the death of environmentalism to the politics of possibility.* Boston: Houghton Mifflin.

Nordhaus, William. 2008. *A question of balance.* Cambridge: MIT Press.

Nordhaus, William, and Joseph Boyer. 2000. *Warming the world: Economic models of global warming.* Cambridge: MIT Press.

Nordlinger, Eric A. 1981. *On the autonomy of the democratic state.* Cambridge: Harvard University Press.

Norton, Bryan G. 1991. *Toward unity among environmentalists.* New York: Oxford University Press.

Norton, Peter D. 2008. *Fighting Traffic: The dawn of the motor age in the American city.* Cambridge: MIT Press.

Notter, Harley. 1949 [1975]. *Postwar foreign policy preparation, 1939–1945.* Washington, DC: U.S. Government Printing Office.

O'Connor, James. 1998. *Natural causes: Essays in ecological Marxism.* New York: Guilford.

———. 2002 (1973). *The fiscal crisis of the state.* New York: Transaction.

O'Connor, Martin, ed. 1994. *Is capitalism sustainable?* New York: Guilford.

Offe, Claus. 1974. Structural problems of the capitalist state: Class rule and the political system on the selectiveness of political institutions. In *German political studies.* Vol. 1, ed. Klaus von Beyme. Beverly Hills: Sage.

———. 1984. *Contradictions of the welfare state.* Cambridge: MIT Press.

Ohmae, Kenichi. 1999. *The borderless world: Power and strategy in the interlinked economy,* 2nd ed. New York: Collins.

Olegario, Rowena. 2006. *A culture of credit: Embedding trust and transparency in American business.* Cambridge: Harvard University Press.

Olien, Diana Davids, and Roger M. Olien. 2002. *Oil in Texas: The Gusher Age, 1895–1945.* Austin: University of Texas Press.

Olien, Roger M., and Diana Davids Olien. 2000. *Oil and ideology: The cultural creation of the American petroleum industry.* Chapel Hill: University of North Carolina Press.

Olney, Martha L. 1989. Credit as a production-smoothing device: The case of automobiles, 1913–1938. *Journal of Economic History* 49, no. 2: 377–91.

———. 1991. *Buy now, pay later: Advertising, credit, and consumer durables in the 1920s.* Chapel Hill: University of North Carolina Press.

Olson, Mancur. 1971 (1965). *The logic of collective action: Public goods and the theory of groups.* Cambridge: Harvard University Press.

Orsi, Richard J. 1985. "Wilderness Saint" and "Robber Baron": The anomalous partnership of John Muir and the Southern Pacific Company for preservation of Yosemite National Park. *Pacific Historian* 29 (Summer-Fall): 136–52.

Pack, Janet Rothenberg, ed. 2005. *Sunbelt/frostbelt: Public policies and market forces in metropolitan development.* Washington, DC: Brookings.

Paehlke, Robert C. 2003. *Democracy's dilemma: Environment, social equity, and the global economy.* Cambridge: MIT Press.

Painter, David S. 1986. *Oil and the American Century: The political economy of U.S. foreign oil policy, 1941–1954.* Baltimore: Johns Hopkins University Press.

Palfreman, Jon. 2006. A tale of two fears: Exploring media depictions of nuclear power and global warming. *Review of Policy Research* 23, no. 1: 23–44.

Parmar, Inderjeet. 1995. The issue of state power: The Council on Foreign Relations as a case study. *Journal of American Studies* 29, no. 1: 73–95.

———. 1999. "Mobilizing America for an internationalist foreign policy": The role of the Council on Foreign Relations. *Studies in American Political Development* 13 (Fall): 337–73.

———. 2002a. American foundations and the development of international knowledge networks. *Global Networks* 2, no. 1: 13–30.

———. 2002b. "To relate knowledge and action": The impact of the Rockefeller Foundation on foreign policy thinking during America's rise to globalism 1939–1945. *Minerva* 40, no. 3: 236–63.

———. 2004. *Think tanks and power in foreign policy: A comparative study of the role and influence of the Council on Foreign Relations and the Royal Institute of International Affairs, 1939–1945*. New York: Palgrave Macmillan.

Parra, Francisco. 2004. *Oil politics: A modern history of petroleum*. New York: I. B. Tauris.

Paterson, Matthew. 2007. *Automobile politics*. New York: Cambridge University Press.

Patterson, Dennis, and Ari Afilalo. 2008. *The new global trading order: The evolving state and the future of trade*. New York: Cambridge University Press.

Pauly Jr., Robert J., and Tom Lansford. 2005. *Strategic preemption: US foreign policy and the second Iraq war*. Burlington, VT: Ashgate.

Paxson, Frederic L. 1946. The American Highway Movement, 1916–1935. *American Historical Review* 51, no. 2: 236–53.

Perelman, Michael. 2003. *The perverse economy*. New York: Palgrave Macmillan.

Pierson, Paul. 2000. Increasing returns, path dependence, and the study of politics. *American Political Science Review* 94, no. 2: 251–67.

Pieterse, Edgar. 2008. *City futures: Confronting the crisis of urban development*. London: Zed Books.

Pieterse, Jen Nederveen. 2004. *Globalization or empire?* New York: Routledge.

Pinderhughes, Raquel. 2004. *Alternative urban futures: Planning for sustainable development in cities throughout the world*. Lanham, MD: Rowman and Littlefield.

Philip, George. 1994. *The political economy of international oil*. Edinburgh: Edinburgh University Press.

Phillips, Don. 2007, June 18. Air Force hopes to cut oil's role in fuel. *New York Times*, C10.

Piven, Frances, and Richard Cloward. 1971. *Regulating the poor*. New York: Random House.

Podobnik, Bruce. 2006. *Global energy shifts: Fostering sustainability in a turbulent age*. Philadelphia: Temple University Press.

Pope, Carl, and Paul Rauber. 2004. *Strategic ignorance: Why the Bush administration is recklessly destroying a century of environmental progress*. San Francisco: Sierra Club.

Portney, Kent E. 2003. *Taking sustainable cities seriously.* Cambridge: MIT Press.

Posturing and abdication. 2008, July 13. *New York Times*, WK11.

Potoski, Matthew. 2001. Clean air federalism: Do states race to the bottom? *Public Administration Review* 61, no. 3: 335–42.

Poulantzas, Nicos. 1973. *Political power and social classes.* London: New Left Books.

Power, Max S. 2008. *America's nuclear wastelands: Politics, accountability, and cleanup.* Pullman: Washington State University Press.

Prasad, Monica. 2006. *The politics of free markets: The rise of neoliberal economic policies in Britain, France, Germany, and the United States.* Chicago: University of Chicago Press.

Pred, Allan. 1966. *The spatial dynamics of U.S. urban-Industrial growth, 1800–1914.* Cambridge: MIT Press.

———. 1980. *Urban growth and city-systems in the United States, 1840–1860.* Cambridge: Harvard University Press.

Press, Daniel. 2002. *Saving open space: The politics of local preservation in California.* Los Angeles: University of California Press.

Preston, Howard L. 1979. *Automobile age Atlanta: The making of a Southern metropolis, 1900–1935.* Athens: University of Georgia Press.

Purdum, Todd. 2000, February 13. Los Angeles tests its limits in quest to grow. *New York Times*, sec. 1, 1.

Rabe, Barry 2004. *Statehouse and greenhouse: The emerging politics of American climate change policy.* Washington, DC: Brookings.

———. 2008. States on steroids: The intergovernmental odyssey of American climate policy, *Review of Policy Research* 25, no. 2: 105–28.

Radford, Gail. 1996. *Modern housing for America: Policy struggles in the New Deal era.* Chicago: University of Chicago Press.

Rajan, Sudhir. 1996. *The enigma of automobility: Democratic politics and pollution control.* Pittsburgh: University of Pittsburgh Press.

Randall, Stephen J. 2005. *United States foreign oil policy since World War I: For profits and security*, 2nd ed. Kingston: McGill-Queen's University Press.

Redefining Progress. 2002, Feb. 22. Letters and Policy Statements: The Johannesburg Summit 2002: A call for action. Washington, DC: Redefining Progress. Available at http://www.redefiningprogress.org/media/letters/020222_bushcall.html.

Resolutions adopted by the Petroleum Industry War Council as pertaining to a petroleum policy for the United States. 1943, December 9. In *A documentary history of the Petroleum Reserves Corporation, 1943–1944: Prepared for the use of Subcommittee on Multinational Corporations of the Committee on Foreign Relations, United States Senate, May 8, 1974.* Washington, DC: U.S. Government Printing Office, 70–71.

Revkin, Andrew C. 2001, June 12. Warming threat requires action now, scientists say. *New York Times*, A12.

———. 2005, Dec. 21. Gas emissions reached high In U.S. in '04. *New York Times*, A30.

———. 2007, March 3. U.S. predicting steady increase for emissions. *New York Times*, A1.

Ricardo, David. 1830. *On the principles of political economy and taxation*. Washington, DC: J. B. Bell.

Rich, Andrew. 2004. *Think tanks, public policy, and the politics of expertise*. New York: Cambridge University Press.

Ringquist, Evan. 1993. *Environmental protection at the state level: Politics and progress in controlling pollution*. Armonk, NY: M. E. Sharpe.

Robbins, William G. 1982. *Lumberjacks and legislators: Political economy of the U.S. lumber industry, 1890–1941*. College Station: Texas A&M University Press.

———. 1994. *Colony and empire: The capitalist transformation of the American West*. Lawrence: University Press of Kansas.

Roberts, J. Timmons. 2007. Globalizing environmental justice. In *Environmental justice and environmentalism*, ed. Ronald Sandler and Phaedra C. Pezzullo. Cambridge: Cambridge University Press.

Roberts, J. Timmons, and Bradley C. Parks. 2007. *A climate of injustice: Global inequality, North-South politics, and climate policy*. Cambridge: MIT Press.

Roberts, Paul. 2004. *The end of oil: On the edge of a perilous new world*. New York: Houghton Mifflin.

———. 2005. Afterward. In *The end of oil: On the edge of a perilous new world*. New York: Houghton Mifflin.

Robinson, William I. 1996. *Promoting polyarchy: Globalization, US intervention, and hegemony*. New York: Cambridge University Press.

———. 2004. *A theory of global capitalism: Production, class, and state in a transnational world*. Baltimore: Johns Hopkins University Press.

Roelofs, Joan. 2003. *Foundations and public policy: The mask of pluralism*. Albany: State University of New York Press.

Rome, Adam. 2001. *The bulldozer in the countryside: Suburban sprawl and the rise of American environmentalism*. New York: Cambridge University Press.

Romero, Simon. 2005, April 30. Oil-rich Norwegians take world's highest gasoline prices in stride. *New York Times*, C1.

Romm, Joseph J. 2004. *The hype about hydrogen: Fact and fiction in the race to save the climate*. Washington, DC: Island Press.

Rose, Fred. 2000. *Coalitions across the class divide: Lessons from the labor, peace, and environmental movements*. Ithaca: Cornell University Press.

Rose, Mark H. 1979. *Interstate: Express highway politics, 1941–1956*. Lawrence: Regents Press of Kansas.

Rose, Mark H., Bruce E. Seely, and Paul F. Barrett. 2006. *The best transportation system in the world: Railroads, trucks, airlines, and American public policy in the twentieth century*. Columbus: Ohio State University Press.

Rosen, Christine M. 1986. *The limits of power: Great fires and the process of city growth in America*. New York: Cambridge University Press.

Rosen, Elliot. 2005. *Roosevelt, the Great Depression, and the economics of recovery*. Charlottesville: University of Virginia Press.

Rosenthal, Elisabeth. 2008, Feb. 8. Studies call biofuels a greenhouse threat. *New York Times*, A9.

Roy, William. 1997. *Socializing capital: The rise of the large industrial corporation in America*. Princeton: Princeton University Press.

Runte, Alfred. 1997. *National Parks: The American experience*, 3d ed. Lincoln: University of Nebraska Press.

Ruth, Matthias, ed. 2006. *Smart growth and climate change: Regional development, infrastructure, and adaptation*. Northampton, MA: Edward Elgar.

Rutledge, Ian. 2005. *Addicted to oil: America's relentless drive for energy security*. New York: I. B. Tauris.

Sabatier, Paul A. 1987. Knowledge, policy-oriented learning, and policy change. *Knowledge: Creation, Diffusion, Utilization* 8, no. 4: 649–92.

———. 1999. *Theories of the policy process*. Boulder: Westview.

Sabin, Paul. 2004. *Crude politics: The California oil market, 1900–1940*. Los Angeles: University of California Press.

Samuelsohn, Darren. 2006, June 9. Climate: White House presses Congress to fund Asia-Pacific Partnership. *Greenwire*.

Sanders, M. Elizabeth. 1981. *The regulation of natural gas: Policy and politics, 1938–1978*. Philadelphia: Temple University Press.

Saward, Michael. 1992. *Co-optive politics and state legitimacy*. Dartmouth: Aldershot.

Schipper, Janine. 2008. *Disappearing Desert:The growth of Phoenix and the culture of sprawl*. Norman: University of Oklahoma Press.

Schlosberg, David. 1999. *Environmental justice and the new pluralism*. New York: Oxford University Press.

Schlozman, Kay L., and John T. Tierney. 1986. *Organized interests and American democracy*. New York: Harper and Row.

Schmidheiny, Stephan, and Federico Zorraquin, with the World Business Council for Sustainable Development. 1996. *Financing change: The financial community, eco-efficiency, and sustainable development*. Cambridge: MIT Press.

Schnattschneider, E. E. 1960. *The semisovereign people*. New York: Holt, Rinehart, and Winston.

Schrepfer, Susan R. 1983. *The fight to save the redwoods: A history of environmental reform, 1917–1978*. Madison: University of Wisconsin Press.

———. 2005. *Nature's altars: Mountains, gender, and American environmentalism*. Lawrence: University Press of Kansas.

Schultz, Stanley K. 1989. *Constructing urban culture: American cities and city planning, 1800—1920*. Philadelphia: Temple University Press.

Schulzinger, Robert D. 1984. *The wise men of foreign affairs: The history of the Council on Foreign Relations*. New York: Columbia University Press.

Schurr, Sam H., and Bruce C. Netschert. 1960. *Energy in the American economy: 1850–1975*. Baltimore: Johns Hopkins University Press.

Seiler, Cotton. 2003. Statist means to individualist ends: Subjectivity, automobility, and the cold war state. *American Studies* 44, no. 3: 5–36.

Sellars, Richard West. 1997. *Preserving nature in the National Parks: A history*. New Haven: Yale University Press.

Sexton, Patricia. 1991. *The war on labor and the Left*. Boulder: Westview.

Shaffer, Ed. 1983. *The United States and the control of world oil*. New York: St. Martin's.

Shaiko, Ronald. 1999. *Voices and echoes for the environment*. New York: Columbia University Press.

Shambaugh, George E. 2004. The power of money: Global capital and policy choices in developing countries. *American Journal of Political Science* 48, no. 2: 281–95.

Shanker, Thom. 2008, Feb. 4. Proposed military spending is highest since WWII. *New York Times*, A10.

———. 2008, Feb. 9. Europe paints Afghan effort with Iraq brush, Gates says. *New York Times*, A6.

Shatzkin, Amy. 2004. Sprawling towards climate change: Connecting U.S. patterns of land development to greenhouse gas emissions. Paper prepared for the ICLEI: Local Governments for Sustainability. Berkeley, CA: ICLEI: Local Governments for Sustainability.

Sheehan, Molly O'Meara. 2001. *City limits: Putting the brakes on sprawl*. Washington, DC: Worldwatch Institute.

Shellenberger, Michael, and Ted Nordhaus. 2004. *The death of environmentalism: Global warming politics in a post-environmental world*. Washington, DC: Michael Shellenberg and Ted Nordhaus.

Shoup, Laurence H. 1974. Shaping the national interest: The Council on Foreign Relations, the Department of State, and the origins of the postwar world, 1939–1943. PhD Thesis, Northwestern University.

Shoup, Laurence H., and William Minter. 1977. *Imperial brain trust: The Council on Foreign Relations and United States foreign policy*. New York: Monthly Review Press.

Shulman, Seth. 2006. *Undermining science: Suppression and distortion in the Bush administration*. Berkeley: University of California Press.

Simmons, Matthew R. 2005. *Twilight in the desert: The coming Saudi oil shock and the world economy*. New York: Wiley.

SIPRI Yearbook 2007: *Armaments, disarmament, and international security. 2007*. New York: Oxford University Press.

Sklair, Leslie. 2001. *The transnational capitalist class*. Malden, MA: Blackwell.

Skocpol, Theda. 1979. *States and social revolutions*. New York: Cambridge University Press.

———. 1985. Bringing the state back in: Strategies of analysis in current research. In *Bringing the state back in*, ed. Peter Evans, Dietrich Rueschemeyer, and Theda Skocpol. New York: Cambridge University Press.

———. 1986/7. A brief response [to G. William Domhoff]. *Politics and Society* 15, no. 3: 331–32.

———. 1992. *Protecting soldiers and mothers: The political origins of social policy in the United States*. Cambridge: Harvard University Press.

Skocpol, Theda, Marshall Ganz, and Ziad Munson. 2000. "A nation of organizers: The institutional origins of civic voluntarism in the United States." *American Political Science Review* 94, no. 3: 527–46.

Skowronek, Stephen. 1982. *Building a new American state: The expansion of national administrative capacities, 1877–1920*. New York: Cambridge University Press.

Sloman, Lynn. 2006. *Car sick: Solutions for our car-addicted culture*. Devon, UK: Green Books.

Smith, Carl. 2006. *The plan of Chicago: Daniel Burnham and the remaking of the American city*. Chicago: University of Chicago Press.

Smith, Eric R. A. N. 2002. *Energy, the environment, and public opinion*. Lanham, MD: Rowman and Littlefield.

Smith, Neil. 2003. *American empire: Roosevelt's geographer and the prelude to globalization*. Berkeley: University of California Press.

Snell, Bradford C. 1974. *American ground transport*. Washington, DC: U.S. Government Printing Office.

Solecki, William, and Charles Oliveri. 2004. Downscaling climate change scenarios in an urban land use change model. *Journal of Environmental Management* 72: 105–15.

Soule, David C. 2006. *Urban sprawl: A comprehensive reference guide*. Westport, CT: Greenwood.

St. Clair, David J. 1986. *The motorization of American cities*. New York: Praeger.

Steele, Brian C. H., and Angelika Heinzel. 2001, November. Materials for fuel-cell technologies. *Nature* 414: 345–52.

Stigler, George J. 1971. The theory of economic regulation. *Bell Journal of Economics and Management Science* 2 (Spring): 3–21.

Stiglitz, Joseph E., and Linda J. Bilmes. 2008. *The three trillion dollar war: The true cost of the Iraq conflict*. New York: Norton.

Stilgoe, John. 1988. *Borderland: Origins of the American suburb, 1820–1939*. New Haven: Yale University Press.

Stilwell, Frank J. B. 2002. *Political economy: The contest of economic ideas*. New York: Oxford University Press.

Stoett, Peter. 2003. Toward renewed legitimacy? Nuclear power, global warming, and security. *Global Environmental Politics* 3, no, 1: 99–116.

Stoff, Michael B. 1980. *Oil, war, and American security: The search for a national policy on foreign oil, 1941–1947*. New Haven: Yale University Press.

Stone, Clarence N. 1989. *Regime politics*. Lawrence: University Press of Kansas.

Stone, Michael E. 1980. The housing problem in the United States: Origins and prospects. *Socialist Review* 52, no. 4: 65–119.

Stradling, David. 1999. *Smokestacks and progressives: Environmentalists, engineers, and air quality in America, 1881–1951*. Baltimore: Johns Hopkins University Press.

Stradling, David, and Joel A. Tarr. 1999. Environmental activism, locomotive smoke, and the corporate response. *Business History Review* 73, no. 4: 677–704.

Strange, Susan. 1996. *The retreat of the state: The diffusion of power in the world economy*. New York: Cambridge University Press.

Szasz, Andrew. 1994. *Ecopopulism*. Minneapolis: University of Minnesota Press.

Tarrow, Sidney. 1994. *Power in movement*. New York: Cambridge University Press.

Tebeau, Mark. 2003. *Eating smoke: Fire in urban America, 1800–1950*. Baltimore: Johns Hopkins University Press.

Tesh, Sylvia Noble. 2000. *Uncertain hazards: Environmental activists and scientific proof*. Ithaca: Cornell University Press.

The chips are down. 2002, April 27. *New Scientist* 174, no. 2340: 30–37.

Thomas, Robert Paul. 1977. *An analysis of the pattern of growth of the automobile industry, 1895–1929*. New York: Arno.

Todd, Emmanuel. 2003. *After the empire: The breakdown of the American order,* trans. C. Jon Delogu. New York: Columbia University Press.

Tonelson, Alan. 2000. *The race to the bottom: Why a worldwide worker surplus and uncontrolled free trade are sinking American living standards.* Boulder: Westview.

Truman, David B. 1951. *The Governmental process: Political interests and public opinion.* New York: Knopf.

Twentieth Century Fund Task Force on the International Oil Crisis. 1975. *Paying for energy.* New York: McGraw-Hill.

Twentieth Century Fund Task Force on United States Energy Policy. 1977. *Providing for energy.* New York: McGraw-Hill.

Uchitelle, Louis. 2006, Dec. 24. Goodbye, production (and maybe innovation). *New York Times,* sec. 3, 4.

United Nations Framework Convention on Climate Change. 2006, Oct. 19. *National greenhouse gas inventory data for the period 1990–2004 and status of reporting.* New York: United Nations.

United States Department of Energy. 2006. *Biomass energy data book.* Washington, DC: United States Department of Energy.

———. 2007. *Transportation energy data book.* Washington, DC: United States Department of Energy.

Useem, Michael. 1984. *The inner circle: Large corporations and the rise of business political activity in the U.S. and U.K.* New York: Oxford University Press.

Uzawa, Hirofumi. 2003. *Economic theory and global warming.* New York: Cambridge University Press.

Vallianatos, Mark, Regina M. Freer, Peter Dreier, and Robert Gottlieb. 2005. *The next Los Angeles: The struggle for a livable city.* Los Angeles: University of California Press.

Van der Pijl, Kees. 1999. *Transnational classes and international relations.* New York: Routledge.

Van Til, Jon. 1982. *Living with Energy Shortfall.* Boulder: Westview.

Vandenbosch, Robert, and Susanne E. Vandenbosch. 2007. *Nuclear waste stalemate: Political and scientific controversies.* Salt Lake City: University of Utah Press.

Viehe, Fred W. 1981. Black gold suburbs: The influence of the extractive industry on the suburbanization of Los Angeles, 1890–1930. *Journal of Urban History* 8, no. 1: 3–26.

Vietor, Richard H. 1980. *Environmental politics and the coal coalition.* College Station: Texas A&M University Press.

———. 1984. *Energy policy in America since 1945.* New York: Cambridge University Press.

Visor, Victor J. 2001. Winning the peace: American planning for a profitable postwar world. *Journal of American Studies* 35, no. 1: 111–26.

Volk, Tyler. 2008. *CO2 rising: The world's greatest environmental challenge.* Cambridge: MIT Press.

Wachs, Martin. 1984. Autos, transit, and the sprawl of Los Angeles: The 1920s. *Journal of the American Planning Association* 50, no. 3: 297–310.

Wainwright, Hilary. 1994. *Arguments for a new Left: Answering the free-market Right.* Cambridge, MA: Blackwell.

Wald, Matthew L. 2003, Nov. 12. Will hydrogen clear the air? Maybe not, say some. *New York Times*, C1.

———. 2005, May 9. When it comes to replacing oil imports, nuclear is no easy option, experts say. *New York Times*, A14.

———. 2006, July 5. The search for new oil sources leads to processed coal. *New York Times*, C1.

———. 2008, Feb. 17. As nuclear waste languishes, expense to U.S. rises. *New York Times*, A22.

———. 2008, Oct. 24. After 35-year lull, nuclear power may be in early stages of a revival. *New York Times*, B3.

Walker, Jack L. 1983, June. The origins and maintenance of interest groups in America. *American Political Science Review*, 77: 390–406.

———. 1991. *Mobilizing interest groups in America*. Ann Arbor: University of Michigan Press.

Walker, Louise Drusilla. 1941. The Chicago Association of Commerce: Its history and policies. PhD Diss., University of Chicago.

Wall, Derek. 1999. *Earth First! and the anti-roads movement: Radical environmentalism and comparative social movements*. New York: Routledge.

Wallerstein, Immanuel Maurice. 1974/1980. *The modern world-system*. Vols. 1–2. New York: Academic Press.

Warner, Kee, and Harvey Molotch. 2000. *Building rules: How local controls shape community environments and economies*. New York: Westview.

Warner, Sam Bass. 1978. *Streetcar suburbs: The process of growth in Boston, 1870–1900*. Cambridge: Harvard University Press.

Weale, Albert. 1992. *The new politics of pollution*. New York: Manchester University Press.

Weaver, John C. 2003. *The great land rush and the making of the modern world, 1650–1900*. Montreal: McGill-Queen's University Press.

Weber, Edward P. 1998. *Pluralism by the rules: Conflict and cooperation in environmental regulation*. Washington, DC: Georgetown University Press.

Weidenbaum, Murray. 2009. *The competition of ideas: The world of the Washington think tanks*. New Brunswick, NJ: Transaction.

Weinstein, James. 1968. *The corporate ideal in the liberal state: 1900–1918*. Boston: Beacon Press.

Weiss, Linda. 1998. *The myth of the powerless state*. Ithaca: Cornell University Press.

———, ed. 2003. *States in the global economy: Bringing domestic institutions back in*. New York: Cambridge University Press.

Weiss, Marc. 1987. *The rise of the community builders: The American real estate industry and urban land planning*. New York: Columbia University Press.

Weisser, Victor, President, California Council for Environmental and Economic Balance. 2000. Interview by author, 13 March, San Francisco. Tape recording.

West, Darrell, and Burdett A. Loomis. 1999. *The sound of money: How political interests get what they want*. New York: Norton.

Wetherly, Paul. 2005. *Marxism and the state: An analytical approach*. New York: Palgrave MacMillan.

Wetherly, Paul, Clyde W. Barrow, and Peter Burnham, eds. 2008. *Class, power, and the state in capitalist society: Essays on Ralph Miliband*. New York: Palgrave MacMillan.

White, Eugene Nelson. 1983. *The regulation and reform of the American banking system, 1900–1929*. Princeton: Princeton University Press.

Whitt, J. Allen. 1982. *Urban elites and mass transportation*. Princeton: Princeton University Press.

Wicker, Elmus. 1996. *The banking panics of the Great Depression*. New York: Cambridge University Press.

Wilbanks, Thomas J. 2006. Stakeholder involvement in local smart growth: Needs and challenges. In *Smart growth and climate change*, ed. Matthias Ruth. Northampton, MA: Edward Elgar.

Wilcox, Ronald T. 2008. *Whatever happened to thrift? Why Americans don't save and what to do about it*. New Haven: Yale University Press.

Williams, Alex. 2008, Feb. 10. Don't let the green grass fool you. *New York Times*, ST1.

Winks, Robin W. 1997. *Laurence S. Rockefeller: Catalyst for conservation*. Washington, DC: Island Press.

Wolbrecht, Christina, and Rodney E. Hero, eds. 2005. *The politics of democratic inclusion*. Philadelphia: Temple University Press.

Wolch, Jennifer, Manuel Pastor Jr., and Peter Drier, eds. 2004. *Up against the sprawl: Public policy and the making of Southern California*. Minneapolis: University of Minnesota Press.

Wood, Ellen Meiksins. 1999. *The origin of capitalism*. New York: Monthly Review Press.

———. 2003. *Empire of capital*. New York: Verso.

World Business Council for Sustainable Development (WBCSD). 2002. *WBCSD sector projects*. Washington, DC: World Business Council for Sustainable Development.

———. 2003. *Energy and climate: The WBCSD's itinerary*. Washington, DC: World Business Council for Sustainable Development.

———. 2004. *Mobility 2030: Meeting the challenge of sustainability*. Washington, DC: World Business Council for Sustainable Development.

———. 2005. *Pathways to 2050: Energy and climate*. Washington, DC: World Business Council for Sustainable Development.

———. 2007. *Policy directions to 2050: Energy and climate*. Washington, DC: World Business Council for Sustainable Development.

World oil demand to peak before supply—BP. 2008, January 16. Reuters.

Wriston, Walter B. 1992. *The twilight of sovereignty: How the information revolution is transforming our world*. New York: Scribners.

Wynne, Brian 1982. *Rationality and ritual: The Windscale inquiry and nuclear decisions in Britain*. Chalfont St. Giles, Bucks., Great Britain: British Society for the History of Science.

Yackee, Jason Webb, and Susan Webb Yackee. 2006. A bias toward business? Assessing interest group influence on the U.S. bureaucracy. *Journal of Politics* 68, no. 128–39.

Yago, Glenn. 1984. *The decline of transit: Urban transportation in German and U.S. cities, 1900–1970.* New York: Cambridge University Press.

Yergin, Daniel. 1991. *The prize: The epic quest for oil, money, and power.* New York: Simon and Schuster.

Yetiv, Steve A. 2004. *Crude awakenings: Global oil security and American foreign policy.* Ithaca: Cornell University Press.

———. 2008. *The absence of grand strategy: The United States in the Persian Gulf, 1972–2005.* Baltimore: Johns Hopkins University Press.

York, Richard, and Eugene A. Rosa. 2003. Key challenges to ecological modernization theory. *Organization & Environment* 16, no. 3: 273–88.

Young, Stephen C., ed. 2000. *The emergence of ecological modernisation: Integrating the environment and the economy?* New York: Routledge.

Zaun, Todd. 2005, March 19. Honda tries to spruce up a stodgy image. *New York Times*, C3.

Zimmerman, Julian H. 1959. *The FHA story in summary, 1934–1959.* Washington, DC: U.S. Federal Housing Administration.

# Index